28 Italian Songs an

of the Seventeenth and Eighteenth Centuries

Based on the Editions by Alessandro Parisotti

Edited by Richard Walters

International Phonetic Alphabet and Translations by Martha Gerhart

ED 4412

ISBN 978-0-634-08292-4

LABORUM
DULCE
LENIMEN

G. SCHIRMER

www.schirmer.com
www.halleonard.com

ALESSANDRO PARISOTTI
AND ARIE ANTICHE

If not for the Ricordi publication *Arie antiche*, the name Alessandro Parisotti (1853-1913) likely would have disappeared from music history. Despite his output as a composer of sacred choral music, it is only *Arie antiche*, in three volumes, for which he is remembered. The Italian musician who collected and edited/realized/arranged then forgotten seventeenth and eighteenth century Italian airs is absent from most sources of music research. Parisotti receives a brief note in *Enciclopedia della musica*. He was born in Rome and lived his entire life there. In 1880 he became secretary of the Accademia di Santa Cecilia, an important Roman center of Italian musical research, activity and education since the seventeenth century. He published a treatise on the physics of acoustics, psychology and esthetics of music in 1911.

Research since the publication of *Arie antiche* has shed new light on the authorship of several arias, noted in the articles in this publication. Even so, credit must be given to Parisotti for finding and choosing songs which have stood the test of time, for creating versions of them that remain beautiful, and for conceiving of a collection that influenced vocal study around the world. Other publications of Baroque Italian songs were released in the late nineteenth century and early to mid-twentieth century, but none had the international impact of *Arie antiche*, or its related Schirmer publications *Anthology of Italian Song of the Seventeenth and Eighteenth Centuries* and *24 Italian Songs and Arias of the Seventeenth and Eighteenth Centuries*.

During the 1870s and '80s, much "modern music" was received with nothing short of vehemence. Composers like Liszt and Wagner, who viewed themselves as writing "music of the future," found themselves greeted with scorn and loathing in some circles. It was in this musical climate that Parisotti compiled a collection of arias from the previous two centuries. In the original preface to *Arie antiche*, Parisotti noted that "music… can readily derive from grand models whatever it may need for the improvement and development of its productions." He acknowledged this as a "paraphrase of the well-known saying of our great modern melodramatist." The towering Italian music figure of the day, Giuseppe Verdi, had made a controversial and widely discussed statement in 1871 that a return to the past would actually be progress.

Parisotti's original preface to *Arie antiche* states:

Since these days the truly new is becoming rarer, I am pleased to see the old resurrected in its place. Composers in the seventeenth and eighteenth centuries wrote music that was enlightened, above all, by structural purity and simplicity, emotion, and a quality of the serenity over the complete piece. The music of today is decidedly the opposite: erratic, jerky and full of violent contrasts.

According to Parisotti, the arias in his collections were "… gleaned from old manuscripts and ancient editions, where they lay in unmerited oblivion. … In transcribing the melodies the utmost care was taken to alter nothing in the originals, and often various manuscripts were consulted to ascertain the elegant and correct form." Of his accompaniments and harmonizations of *basso continuo* he noted, "care was taken to insert nothing out of keeping with the words or character of the compositions, or with the style of the author and his period."

The original credit on the *Arie antiche* collection reads "Raccolte ed elaborate da A. Parisotti" (collected and elaborated by A. Parisotti). His source was generally a vocal melody and a figured bass, though for some selections he used previously published nineteenth century realizations/editions which he credited (later removed), particularly those by François Auguste Gevaert and Carl Banck, whose credits are cited in this edition.

Clearly, late nineteenth century ideas of musical objectivity are different from a current view. The Romanticism of Parisotti's period is inescapably part of the style of his editions. His late nineteenth century approach to Baroque music is in itself historical. Musicology was in its infancy in the nineteenth century, particularly in Italy. A concept of early music performance practice did not exist. Parisotti arranged piano accompaniments to support the forgotten melodies he discovered and edited, making the songs comprehensible in style to singers and audiences of the Italian salon song era. Nationalism was also strong in the years following the creation of the unified Italian republic in 1870, and interest in historical Italian song was part of the temper of the times.

Based on his work on *Arie antiche* and the song "Se tu m'ami," attributed to Pergolesi but now presumed to have been a Parisotti original composition, Parisotti was a very good composer and arranger. His realizations/editions of these Baroque songs sound like the fresh work of an inquisitive young man in love with the arias, the voice, and the piano. His accompaniments were written for a modern pianoforte, and are satisfying on the instrument in a way that a purer, more restrained early music approach to realization is not. Though other points of view, reflecting mid to late twentieth century values of Baroque performance practice, have been made to this music since, Parisotti's versions remain musically convincing on their own terms, and are preferred by many singers and teachers.

Added vocal ornamentation is certainly possible in this music beyond Parisotti's suggestions, and is encouraged if tasteful in style. Further suggested ornamentation was outside the purpose of this edition, a fresh presentation of Parisotti's familiar editions, plus the four songs from *24 Italian Songs and Arias of the Seventeenth and Eighteenth Centuries* not edited by Parisotti.

Research sources for this edition were numerous. John Glenn Paton's enlightening research on these songs and arias deserves mention.

Comments on the original 24 Italian Songs and Arias
of the Seventeenth and Eighteenth Centuires

Schirmer originally published *24 Italian Songs and Arias of the Seventeenth and Eighteenth Centuries* in 1948, compiled by Lester Hodges. Most of the contents were assembled from the previously released Schirmer publication *Anthology of Italian Song of the Seventeenth and Eighteenth Centuries*, originally released in 1894. The source for this publication was *Arie antiche*, edited by Alessandro Parisotti, published in three volumes by Ricordi beginning in 1885.

Richard Walters
editor
May, 2008

CONTENTS

CONTENTS ALPHABETICALLY BY TITLE

About the IPA Transliterations

While the use of the International Phonetic Alphabet (IPA) has become a familiar learning tool for singers, details about choices in IPA transliterations differ among published diction manuals and other publications. Following is a brief explanation of how the IPA transliterations have been done for this publication:

Format:
- The division of syllables is indicated by a space, and the sign ['] precedes the stressed syllable.
- The colon sign [:] is used only to indicate double consonants.

Content and justification:
- I am transliterating all unstressed "e's" and "o's" as closed, as in the highest (Tuscan) spoken form of the language, and as printed in the 11th edition of the authoritative Italian dictionary *Vocabolario della lingua italiana* edited by Nicola Zingarelli. In practice, singers will, for acceptable reasons, alter the degree of "closed" or "open" "e" and "o" vowels in both unstressed and stressed positions.
- I am using the "eng" [ŋ] as the preferred sound before a hard "g" or "k" sound. However, the singer who chooses to use the frontal "n" in its place will not be incorrect, as long as no "shadow vowel" results in its execution.
- I am not using the nasal "m" symbol [ɱ] when the letter "n" assimilates before "b," "p," "m," "f," or "v." While this is an important sophistication of Italian diction, I felt that its use could be unnecessarily confusing to the student who would wonder why "un" (as in "un bel dì") was transliterated as [um], unlike in any dictionary.
- Neither am I transcribing spellings for syntactical (phrasal) doubling by which, for example, "ah, sì" becomes [as: 'si]. Students will incorporate this important sophistication of pronunciation with discretion and, best, upon the advice of experts.
- The intervocalic "s" is unvoiced in some Italian words in the spoken form; hence the word "così," for instance, is in the dictionary as [ko 'si]. However, in practice, in the interest of legato, such "s's" are usually sung as voiced, and therefore I am transliterating them as such.

Pronunciation Key

IPA Symbol	Approximate sound in English	IPA Symbol	Approximate sound in English
[i]	f<u>ee</u>t	[s]	<u>s</u>et
[e]	pot<u>a</u>to	[z]	<u>z</u>ip
[ɛ]	b<u>e</u>d	[l]	<u>l</u>ip
[a]	f<u>a</u>ther	[ʎ]	mil<u>li</u>on
[ɔ]	t<u>au</u>t		
[o]	t<u>o</u>te	[ɾ]	as British "very" – flipped "<u>r</u>"
[u]	t<u>u</u>be	[r]	no English equivalent – rolled "r"
[j]	<u>Y</u>ale		
[w]	<u>w</u>atch	[n]	<u>n</u>ame
		[m]	<u>m</u>op
[b]	<u>b</u>eg	[ŋ]	a<u>n</u>chor
[p]	<u>p</u>et	[ɲ]	o<u>ni</u>on
[d]	<u>d</u>eep	[tʃ]	<u>ch</u>eese
[t]	<u>t</u>op	[dʒ]	<u>G</u>eorge
[g]	<u>G</u>ordon	[dz]	feed<u>s</u>
[k]	<u>k</u>it	[ts]	fi<u>ts</u>
[v]	<u>v</u>et		
[f]	<u>f</u>it	[:]	indicates doubled consonants
[ʃ]	<u>sh</u>e	[']	indicates the primary stress; the syllable following the mark is stressed

—Martha Gerhart

28 Italian Songs and Arias

of the Seventeenth and Eighteenth Centuries

O leggiadri occhi belli

Anonymous, 17th century

"O leggiadri occhi belli" appeared in Parisotti's *Arie antiche* Volume 3, in the key of A-flat major. In his introductory notes Parisotti states that he found his source at the Biblioteca Nazionale in Florence among other manuscripts, some by Monteverdi. Parisotti speculates that based on style the composer is Andrea Falconieri (1585 or 1586-1656), but this has not been substantiated.

o	led: ˈdʒa dri	ˈɔk: ki	ˈbɛl: li	ˈɔk: ki	ˈmjɛ i	ˈka ɾi
O	**leggiadri**	**occhi**	**belli,**	**occhi**	**miei**	**cari,**
o	lovely	eyes	beautiful	eyes	mine	dear

O beautiful lovely eyes, my dear eyes,

ˈvi vi	ˈrad: dʒi	del	tʃɛl	se ˈre ni	e	ˈkja ɾi
vivi	**raggi**	**del**	**ciel**	**sereni**	**e**	**chiari,**
bright	rays	of the	sky	serene	and	clear

bright rays serene and clear as the sky,

po i ˈke	ˈtan to	bra ˈma te	di	ve ˈder mi	laŋ ˈgwi ɾe	di	ve ˈder mi	mo ˈri ɾe
poiché	**tanto**	**bramate**	**di**	**vedermi**	**languire,**	**di**	**vedermi**	**morire,**
since	so much	you desire	of	to see me	to languish	of	to see me	to die

since you desire so much to see me languish, to see me die,

ˈɔk: ki	ˈbɛl: li	ke	a ˈdo ɾo	mi ˈɾa te	ˈki o	ˈmɔ ɾo
occhi	**belli**	**che**	**adoro,**	**mirate**	**ch'io**	**moro.**
eyes	beautiful	that	I adore	look at	that I	I die

beautiful eyes I adore, look: I am dying.

o	se ˈre ne	ˈmi e	ˈlu tʃi	o	ˈlu tʃi	a ˈma te
O	**serene**	**mie**	**luci,**	**o**	**luci**	**amate,**
o	serene	my	eyes	o	eyes	loved

O my serene eyes, o beloved eyes,

ˈtan to	ˈkru de	al	ˈmi o	a ˈmor	ˈquan to	spje ˈta te
tanto	**crude**	**al**	**mio**	**amor**	**quanto**	**spietate,**
so much	cruel	to the	my	love	as much	pitiless

as cruel to my love as pitiless,

po i ˈke	ˈtan to	go ˈde te	ˈdel: la	ˈfjam: ma	ˈki o	ˈsɛn to
poiché	**tanto**	**godete**	**della**	**fiamma**	**ch'io**	**sento**
since	so much	you enjoy	of the	flame	that I	I feel

del	ˈmi o	ˈgra ve	tor ˈmen to
del	**mio**	**grave**	**tormento,**
of the	my	grave	torment

since you enjoy so much the flame I feel in my deep torment,

dɛ	mi ˈɾa te mi	un	ˈpɔ ko	e	dʒo ˈi te	al	ˈmi o	ˈfɔ ko
deh	**miratemi**	**un**	**poco**	**e**	**gioite**	**al**	**mio**	**foco.**
ah	look at me	a	little	and	have pleasure	at the	my	fire

ah, look at me a little and take pleasure from my fire.

O leggiadri occhi belli

Anonymous

Anonymous, 17th century
edited and realized by
Alessandro Parisotti

mor quan-to spie-ta - te, poi-ché tan-to go-

de - te del-la fiam-ma ch'io sen - to

del mio gra-ve tor-men - to, deh mi-ra-te-mi un

po-co e gio - i-te al mio fo-co, gio - i-te al mio fo - co.

Nina

Anonymous
previously attributed to Giovanni Battista Pergolesi

"Nina" was first heard in London in 1749. It has been variously attributed to Giovanni Battista Pergolesi, Legrenzio Vincenzo Ciampi and Rinaldo di Capua, but twentieth century research disputes these attributions and no composer has been credited. The aria remains a mystery. Attribution to Pergolesi was not uncommon in the eighteenth century. During Pergolesi's short lifetime he attained little success, but following his death was recognized as a leader in Italian comic opera. He became revered throughout Europe for the opera *La serva padrona,* which by 1755 had been performed 200 times in Paris. The *Stabat Mater* grew to enormous popularity as well. Little was known about the Italian composer that had died so young. By mid-eighteenth century Pergolesi's name had such appeal that sometimes impresarios and publishers credited him with scores by various and unknown composers in order to draw audience and sales. The practice later extended to small instrumental works. The name "Pergolesi" nearly became a catch-all for any anonymous work of the eighteenth century, and many spurious publications resulted with that attribution.

"Nina" was included in a 1749 British publication *The Favourite Songs in the Opera called Li tre cicisbei ridicoli,* attributed to Pergolesi but almost surely not by him, but rather a compilation of pieces by various unknown composers.

In a 1949 article in *Music and Letters* Frank Walker states:

'Tre giorni son che Nina' was attributed generally to Pergolesi until Spitta, in 1887, claimed it for Rinaldo di Capua, on the grounds that it appeared in *La Bohémienne,* a French adaptation of Rinald's *La zingara,* performed in Paris in 1755. Barclay Squire demolished Spitta's claim for Rinaldo by demonstrating that the song was introduced into La *Bohmémienne* from a comic opera, *Li tre cicisbei ridicoli,* performed in London in 1749. This opera, first produced at Bologna in 1748 and revived at Venice in 1748 and 1752, is by the obscure Milanese composer Natale Resta. 'Tre giorni,' however, does not appear in the librettos of either the Bologna or the Venice performances. It seems certain that it was introduced into Resta's *Li tre cicisbei ridicoli* by Vincenzo Ciampi, who was maestro to the opera company responsible for the London performances. But that is not to say that the song was composed by Ciampi. It is used as a serenade by one of the characters in the opera, with a second verse which does not appear in any of the MS versions of the song. There is no character called Nina in *Li tre cicisbei ridicoli.* It seems likely that 'Tre giorni' was a popular song, possibly but by no means certainly composed by Pergolesi, familiar to Ciampi from his Neapolitan days, and introduced by him into Resta's opera in London, with the addition of a second verse to give it some connection with the plot.

"Nina" did not appear in Parisotti's *Arie antiche.* It was published by Schirmer as early as 1904, but the source is unknown. It was later included in the 1948 Schirmer publication *24 Italian Songs and Arias of the Seventeenth and Eighteenth Centuries.*

tre	ˈdʒor ni	son	ke	ˈni na	in	ˈlɛt: to	se ne ˈsta
Tre	**giorni**	**son**	**che**	**Nina**	**in**	**letto**	**se ne sta.**
three	days	are	that	Nina	in	bed	herself stays

For three days Nina has been in bed.

ˈpif: fe ɾi	ˈtim pa ni	ˈtʃem ba li	zveʎ: ˈʎa te	ˈmi a	ni ˈnet: ta
Pifferi,	**timpani,**	**cembali,**	**svegliate**	**mia**	**Ninetta,**
fifes	drums	cymbals	awaken	my	dear Nina

Fifes, drums, cymbals, awaken my dear Nina,

at: ˈtʃɔ	non	ˈdɔr ma	pju
acciò	**non**	**dorma**	**più.**
so that	not	she may sleep	more

so that she will sleep no longer.

Nina

Anonymous

Anonymous

Tre _ gior - ni son che Ni - na, che Ni - na, che

Ni - na in let - to se ne sta, _____ in _ let - to _ se ne

sta. Pif - fe-ri, tim - pa-ni, cem - ba-li, sve - glia _ te mia Ni -

*optional introduction chord

Pietà, Signore!

Anonymous
previously attributed to
Alessandro Stradella
(1639-1682)

The origins of "Pietà signore" are not clear. In his edition of this song, John Glenn Paton states that the probable composer is François Joseph Fétis, who in 1843 published the song with the words "Pietà, Signore!," attributing it to Stradella. This music had been published in Paris in 1838 with the words "Se i miei sospiri." No manuscript was ever found, and there is nothing in the style of the piece to link it to Stradella. The true composer is unknown. Paton speculates that Fétis created a hoax by claiming that Stradella wrote the music. That may be true, but it is probably impossible to prove conclusively.

Whatever its origins, "Pietà, Signore!" became popular in the nineteenth century, and has been part of the Italian song teaching repertory ever since. The song does not appear in Parisotti's *Arie antiche*. It was first published by Schirmer in 1914 (source unknown), and was included in Lester Hodges' Schirmer 1948 compilation *24 Italian Songs and Arias of the Seventeenth and Eighteenth Centuries*.

pje 'ta siɲ: 'ɲo ɾe di me do 'lɛn te siɲ: 'ɲor pje 'ta
Pietà, Signore, di me, dolente! Signor, pietà,
pity Lord on me suffering Lord pity
Have pity, Lord, on suffering me! Lord, have pity,

se a te 'dʒun dʒe il 'mi o pre 'gar non mi pu 'ni ska il 'tu o ri 'gor
se a te giunge il mio pregar. Non mi punisca il tuo rigor;
if to you reaches the my praying not me may punish the your severity
if my praying reaches you. May your severity not punish me;

'me no se 've ɾi kle 'mɛn ti oɲ: 'ɲo ɾa 'vɔl dʒi i 'two i 'zgwar di 'so pra di me
meno severi, clementi ognora, volgi i tuoi sguardi sopra di me.
less severe merciful always turn the your glances over of me
less stern, always merciful, turn your gaze upon me.

non 'fi a 'ma i ke nel: lin 'fɛr no 'si a dan: 'na to
Non fia mai che nell'inferno sia dannato
not it may be ever that in the hell I may be damned
May it never be that in hell I am damned

nel 'fwɔ ko e 'tɛr no dal 'tu o ri 'gor
nel fuoco eterno dal tuo rigor.
in the fire eternal by the your severity
to the eternal fire by your severity.

gran 'di o dʒam: 'ma i 'si a dan: 'na to nel 'fwɔ ko e 'tɛr no dal 'tu o ri 'gor
Gran Dio, giammai sia dannato nel fuoco eterno dal tuo rigor.
great God never I may be damned in the fire eternal by the your severity
Great God, may I never be damned to the eternal fire by your severity.

pje 'ta siɲ: 'ɲo ɾe siɲ: 'ɲor pje 'ta di me do 'lɛn te
Pietà, Signore, Signor, pietà di me dolente,
pity Lord Lord pity on me suffering
Have pity, Lord; Lord, have pity on suffering me,

se a te 'dʒun dʒe il 'mi o pre 'ga ɾe
se a te giunge il mio pregare.
if to you reaches the my praying
if my praying reaches you.

'me no se 've ɾi kle 'mɛn ti oɲ: 'ɲo ɾa 'vɔl dʒi i 'zgwar di
Meno severi, clementi ognora, volgi i sguardi,
less severe merciful always turn the glances
Less stern, always merciful, turn your gaze;

dɛ 'vɔl dʒi i 'zgwar di su me siɲ: 'ɲor
deh volgi i sguardi su me, Signor.
please turn the glances on me Lord
please turn your gaze upon me, Lord.

Pietà, Signore!

Anonymous

Anonymous

Non posso disperar
from the opera *Eraclea*

Giovanni Bononcini
(1670-1747)

Composer Giovanni Bononcini, cellist and composer, was the son of Italian violinist and composer Giovanni Maria Bononcini. Born in Modena, he studied in Bologna, where he was later accepted into the Accademia Filarmonica, and became *maestro di cappella* at San Giovanni in Monte in 1687. Two years later he left the post, and worked on commissions and as a freelance musician until settling in Rome in 1692. In the next four years there, in service to Filippo Colonna, Bononcini composed five operas, an oratorio and several serenatas with librettist Silvio Stampiglia. *Il trionfo di Camilla*, a 1696 opera from this period, astounded audiences in its Naples premiere with its inventive melodies. Within the next five years the opera was produced in 14 other Italian cities. After the death of his patron, Bononcini moved to Vienna in 1697 where he was in service to Leopold I. By 1705 the composer's music was known throughout Europe, and his international success continued for years after that, with Bononcini working in various locations on the continent. Between 1720 and 1732 Bononcini worked in London, where his operas rivaled Handel in popularity. His later works, after 1732, were primarily written for Paris, Lisbon and Vienna. Both Giovanni Bononcini and his half-brother, Antonio Maria Bononcini, were opera composers.

Eraclea was a pasticcio opera with music by Bononcini, first performed in Rome at the Teatro di Tordinona on Janary 12, 1692. It included at least 20 arias, most pre-existing, by Bononcini, loosely woven into a thin plot. In his notes on "Non posso disperar" in *Arie antiche*, Parisotti notes that the arietta was "discovered among old manuscripts of the seventeenth century..." His source cited no composer. Giving composition credit to S. DeLuca, he continues, "despite most patient research, it was impossible to obtain data concerning this composer, who is ignored by the biographers of musicians." Later research has revealed that the aria was composed by Bononcini.

"Non posso disperar" appeared in Parisotti's *Arie antiche* Volume 2, published by Ricordi in 1890, in the key of E minor. Parisotti's metronomic suggestion was quarter note = 80, a tempo reflecting the romantic age of the edition and significantly slower than is commonly performed today. Parisotti's edition was published by G. Schirmer in 1894 in the *Anthology of Italian Song of the Seventeenth and Eighteenth Centuries*, later included in the 1948 Schirmer compilation *24 Italian Songs and Arias of the Seventeenth and Eighteenth Centuries*.

non	'pɔs: so	di spe 'rar	'sɛ i	'trɔp: po	'ka ɾa	al	kɔr
Non	**posso**	**disperar,**	**sei**	**troppo**	**cara**	**al**	**cor.**
not	I am able	to despair	you are	too	dear	to the	heart

I cannot despair; you are too dear to my heart.

il	'so lo	spe 'ra ɾe	da 'ver	a	dʒo 'i ɾe
Il	**solo**	**sperare**	**d'aver**	**a**	**gioire**
the	only	hoping	of to have	to	to enjoy

Just the hope of having joy

mɛ	un	'dol tʃe	laŋ 'gwi ɾe	mɛ	uŋ	'ka ɾo	do 'lor	a	si
m'è	**un**	**dolce**	**languire,**	**m'è**	**un**	**caro**	**dolor,**	**ah,**	**sì!**
to me is	a	sweet	languishing	to me is	a	dear	sadness	ah	yes

is for me a sweet languishing, is for me a dear sadness – ah, yes!

Non posso disperar

Silvio Stampiglia

Giovanni Bononcini
edited and realized by
Alessandro Parisotti

Andante grazioso

*optional introduction chord

Per la gloria d'adorarvi
from the opera *Griselda*

Giovanni Bononcini
(1670-1747)

Composer Giovanni Bononcini, cellist and composer, was the son of Italian violinist and composer Giovanni Maria Bononcini. Born in Modena, he studied in Bologna, where he was later accepted into the Accademia Filarmonica, and became *maestro di cappella* at San Giovanni in Monte in 1687. Two years later he left the post, and worked on commissions and as a freelance musician until settling in Rome in 1692. In the next four years there, in service to Filippo Colonna, Bononcini composed five operas, an oratorio and several serenatas with librettist Silvio Stampiglia. *Il trionfo di Camilla*, a 1696 opera from this period, astounded audiences in its Naples premiere with its inventive melodies. Within the next five years the opera was produced in 14 other Italian cities. After the death of his patron, Bononcini moved to Vienna in 1697 where he was in service to Leopold I. By 1705 the composer's works were known throughout Europe, and his international success continued for years after that, with Bononcini working in various locations on the continent.

Italian opera was in fashion in London by Bononcini's arrival there in 1720. *Griselda*, from which "Per la gloria d'adorarvi" is excerpted, was the fifth of ten operas by the composer performed in London between 1720 and 1732, rivaling the popularity of Handel. Both Giovanni Bononcini and his half-brother, Antonio Maria Bononcini, wrote operas entitled *Griselda*. Antonio's *Griselda* (1718) used a libretto by Apostolo Zeno. Giovanni used Zeno's plot in a new libretto by Paolo Antonio Rolli for his opera, which was premiered at the Haymarket Theatre in London on February 22, 1722. "Per la gloria d'adorarvi" was among the best known Bononcini arias of the day, and was reprinted in Richard Neale's *A Pocket Companion for Gentlemen and Ladies* (1724) and *The British Musical Miscellany* (1735).

"Per la gloria d'adorarvi" appeared in Parisotti's *Arie antiche* Volume 2, published in 1890 by Ricordi, in the key of F major. Parisotti's metronomic suggestion was quarter note = 80, a tempo reflecting the romantic age of the edition and significantly slower than is commonly performed today. Parisotti's edition was published by G. Schirmer in 1894 in the *Anthology of Italian Song of the Seventeenth and Eighteenth Centuries*, later included in the 1948 Schirmer compilation *24 Italian Songs and Arias of the Seventeenth and Eighteenth Centuries*.

per la 'glɔ rja da do 'rar vi 'vɔʎ: ʎo a 'mar vi o 'lu tʃi 'ka ɾe
Per la gloria d'adorarvi voglio amarvi, o luci care.
for the glory of to adore you I want to love you o eyes dear
For the glory of adoring you I want to love you, o dear eyes.

a 'man do pe ne 'rɔ ma 'sɛm pre va me 'rɔ si nel 'mi o pe 'na ɾe
Amando penerò, ma sempre v'amerò, sì, nel mio penare.
loving I will suffer but always you I will love yes in the my suffering
In loving I will suffer; but always I will love you, yes, in my suffering.

pe ne 'rɔ va me 'rɔ 'lu tʃi 'ka ɾe
Penerò, v'amerò, luci care.
I will suffer you I will love eyes dear
I will suffer, I will love you, dear eyes.

'sɛn tsa 'spɛ me di di 'lɛt: to 'va no af: 'fɛt: to ɛ so spi 'ra ɾe
Senza speme di diletto vano affetto è sospirare,
without hope of pleasure futile affection is yearning
Without the hope of pleasure yearning is a futile affection;

ma i 'vɔ stri 'dol tʃi 'ra i ki va ɡed: 'dʒar pwɔ 'ma i e non va 'ma ɾe
ma i vostri dolci rai chi vagheggiar può mai e non v'amare?
but the your sweet eyes who to gaze at is able ever and not you to love
but who can ever gaze at your sweet eyes and not love you?

pe ne 'rɔ va me 'rɔ 'lu tʃi 'ka ɾe
Penerò, v'amerò, luci care!
I will suffer you I will love eyes dear
I will suffer, I will love you, dear eyes!

Per la gloria d'adorarvi

Paolo Antonio Rolli

Giovanni Bononcini
edited and realized by
Alessandro Parisotti

sì, _____ nel mio _____ pe-na - re. Pe - ne - rò, v'a - me - rò,

lu - ci ca - re, pe - ne - rò, v'a - me - rò, lu - ci ca -

re.

Sen - za spe - me di _____ di -

ma i vo-stri dol-ci ra - i chi __ va-gheg-giar può mai __ e

non, __ e non __ v'a-ma - re? Pe - ne-rò, v'a - me-rò, lu-ci ca -

re, pe - ne-rò, v'a - me-rò, lu-ci ca - re!

Amarilli
from the collection *Le nuove musiche*

Giulio Caccini
(1551-1618)

A tenor, composer and instrumentalist, Giulio Caccini was a Medici court musician for much of his life. He was born in either Rome or Tivoli. Around the age of ten he moved to Florence for musical study after his talent was discovered by Cosimo I de' Medici, and became a noted singer at court, known throughout his career for the sweet purity and legato of his tenor voice. He became a foremost teacher of voice. Caccini was part of the informal academy called the Camerata in the 1580s, where his ideas of a speaking style of noble singing earned him the fame of being the inventor of *stile recitativo*. His *Euridice* (composed and published in 1600, first performed in 1602) was one of the first operas ever composed and the first to be published. (Caccini's younger brother Jacopo Peri also wrote an opera in the same year with the same title, the earliest surviving complete opera score. There was sibling rivalry to complete the first opera.)

Beyond *Euridice*, the composer earned his place in music history with the publication of two collections of solo madrigals and airs, *Le nuove musiche* (1601/2), in which "Amarilli" appears; the song was composed sometime before 1600. The publication included an essay by the composer of historical importance on composition and performance in the new monodic style. Another similar collection, *Nuove musiche e nuova maniera di scriverle*, was published in 1614. Caccini was better known as a performer and teacher than as a composer. Despite his claims of having invented the recitative style of dramatic declamation in opera, his most notable contributions to the operatic genre seem to have been in the area of teaching singers to move the emotions of their listeners. He demanded that singers limit their use of ornamentation to the role of text enhancement, and in *Le nuove musiche* wrote out his ideas of proper ornamentation.

"Amarilli" must have found some resonance with audiences immediately, as it was transcribed for virginals in 1603, and was published in an English collection of realizations for lute in 1610. "Amarilli" appeared in Parisotti's *Arie antiche* Volume 2, published in 1890 by Ricordi, in the key of G minor. Parisotti's metronomic suggestion was quarter note = 66, a tempo reflecting the romantic age of the edition and significantly slower than is commonly performed today. With the slightly extended title "Amarilli, mia bella" Parisotti's edition was published by G. Schirmer in 1894 in the *Anthology of Italian Song of the Seventeenth and Eighteenth Centuries*, later included in the 1948 Schirmer compilation *24 Italian Songs and Arias of the Seventeenth and Eighteenth Centuries*.

a ma ˈɾilː li   ˈmi a   ˈbɛlː la
Amarilli,   **mia**   **bella,**
Amarilli   my   beautiful one
Amarilli, my beautiful one,

non   ˈkre di   o   del   ˈmi o   kɔr   ˈdol tʃe de ˈzi o
non   **credi,**   o   **del**   **mio**   **cor**   **dolce** **desio,**
not   you believe o of the my   heart sweet   desire
do you not believe, o sweet desire of my heart,

ˈdɛsː ser tu   la ˈmor   ˈmi o
d'esser   **tu**   **l'amor**   **mio?**
of to be you the love mine
that you are my love?

ˈkre di lo pur   e   se ti ˈmor tasː ˈsa le du bi ˈtar non ti   ˈva le
Credilo **pur:**   **e** **se** **timor** **t'assale,**   **dubitar** **non** **ti**   **vale.**
believe it indeed and if fear   you assails doubting not to you is worth
Do believe it; and if fear assails you, doubting will not avail you.

ˈa pri mi il   ˈpɛtː to e   ve ˈdra i   ˈskritː to iŋ ˈkɔ re
Aprimi **il**   **petto** **e**   **vedrai**   **scritto** **in** **core:**
open me the breast and you will see written in heart
Open my breast and you will see written on my heart:

a ma ˈɾilː li ɛ   il   ˈmi o a ˈmo re
Amarilli **è** **il**   **mio** **amore.**
Amarilli is the my   love
"Amarilli is my love."

Amarilli

(Giovanni) Battista Guarini

Giulio Caccini
edited and realized by
Alessandro Parisotti

Moderato affettuoso

A-ma-ril-li, mia bel-la, non cre-di, o del mio

cor dol - ce de-si - o, d'es - ser tu _____ l'a-mor mi - o? Cre - di-lo pur: e se ti -

*optional introduction chord

Alma del core
from the opera *La costanza in amor vince l'ingann*

Antonio Caldara
(c1670-1736)

One of the most productive composers of his era, Antonio Caldara began his musical career as a cellist. As a boy Antonio sang in the choir of St. Mark's in his native Venice, and in his musical studies there learned viol, cello and keyboard. Giovanni Legrenzi was *maestro di cappella* at St. Mark's in these years; Caldara was certainly influenced by him. Caldara began publishing works soon after the age of 20, and by 30 was an opera composer. Beginning in 1699, for approximately eight years he was in service to Ferdinando Carlo. After some travels and performances in Spain and time in Rome and other places related to commissions, he settled in Vienna in 1716, where for twenty years until his death he served as vice-Kapellmeister to Emporer Charles VI, a position with a handsome salary which required him to compose over 30 dramatic works.

"Alma del core" is from in Caldara's opera *La costanza in amor vince l'inganno*, a 1710 revision of *Opera pastorale* premiered in Mantua in 1701. *La costanza in amor vince l'inganno* was first performed in Macerata in 1710, and in Rome in 1711 coupled with the intermezzo *Pimpinone e Vespetta*. Though "Alma del core" does not appear in *Arie antiche*, Parisotti noted in prefatory material in reference to another aria from the opera ("Sebben, crudele") that the plot of the *La costanza in amor vince l'inganno* is "simple and perfectly idyllic, but the graces of song are lavished throughout with a prodigal hand."

"Alma del core" did not appear in the Schirmer 1894 publication *Anthology of Italian Song of the Seventeenth and Eighteenth Centuries*, nor in its 1926 revised version. Its first Schirmer publication appears to have been in 1948 in *24 Italian Songs and Arias of the Seventeenth and Eighteenth Centuries*, compiled by Lester Hodges. His source was *Alte Meister des Bel Canto*, published by Peters in 1914, edited by Ludwig Landshoff.

'al ma	del	'kɔ ɾe	'spir to	deːˈlal ma	'sɛm pre	ko 'stan te	ta do ɾe 'rɔ
Alma	**del**	**core,**	**spirto**	**dell'alma,**	**sempre**	**costante**	**t'adorerò.**
soul	of the	heart	spirit	of the soul	always	constant	you I will adore

Soul of my heart, spirit of my soul, I will always faithfully adore you.

sa 'ɾɔ	kon 'tɛn to	nel	'mi o	tor 'men to
Sarò	**contento**	**nel**	**mio**	**tormento,**
I will be	content	in the	my	torment

I will be content, in my torment,

se	kwel	bɛl	'lab: bro	ba 'tʃar	po 'trɔ
se	**quel**	**bel**	**labbro**	**baciar**	**potrò.**
if	that	beautiful	lip	to kiss	I will be able

if I will be able to kiss those beautiful lips.

Alma del core

Anonymous

Antonio Caldara
edited by Ludwig Landshoff
and Lester Hodges

Sebben, crudele
from the opera *La costanza in amor vince l'inganno*

Antonio Caldara
(c1670-1736)

One of the most productive composers of his era, Antonio Caldara began his musical career as a cellist. As a boy Antonio sang in the choir of St. Mark's in his native Venice, and in his musical studies there learned viol, cello and keyboard. Giovanni Legrenzi was *maestro di cappella* at St. Mark's in these years; Caldara was certainly influenced by him. Caldara began publishing works soon after the age of 20, and by 30 was an opera composer. Beginning in 1699, for approximately eight years he was in service to Ferdinando Carlo. After some travels and performances in Spain and time in Rome and other places related to commissions, he settled in Vienna in 1716, where for twenty years until his death he served as vice-Kapellmeister to Emporer Charles VI, a position with a handsome salary which required him to compose over 30 dramatic works.

"Sebben, crudele" is from in Caldara's opera *La costanza in amor vince l'inganno*, a 1710 revision of *Opera pastorale* premiered in Mantua in 1701. *La costanza in amor vince l'inganno* was first performed in Macerata in 1710, and in Rome in 1711 coupled with the intermezzo *Pimpinone e Vespetta*. In *Arie antiche*, Parisotti noted that the plot of the *La costanza in amor vince l'inganno* is "simple and perfectly idyllic, but the graces of song are lavished throughout with a prodigal hand."

"Sebben, crudele" appeared in Parisotti's *Arie antiche* Volume 1, published by Ricordi in 1885, in the key of D minor. Parisotti's metronomic suggestion was quarter note = 84, a tempo reflecting the romantic age of the edition and slower than is commonly performed today. Parisotti's edition was published by G. Schirmer in 1894 in the *Anthology of Italian Song of the Seventeenth and Eighteenth Centuries*, later included in the 1948 Schirmer compilation *24 Italian Songs and Arias of the Seventeenth and Eighteenth Centuries*.

seb: ˈbɛn	kru ˈdɛ le	mi	ˈfa i	laŋ ˈgwir	ˈsɛm pre	fe ˈde le	ti	ˈvɔʎː ʎo	a ˈmar
Sebben,	**crudele,**	**mi**	**fai**	**languir,**	**sempre**	**fedele**	**ti**	**voglio**	**amar.**
although	cruel one	me	you make	to languish	always	faithful	you	I want	to love

Although, cruel one, you make me languish, I will always love you faithfully.

kon	la	luŋ ˈget: tsa	del	ˈmi o	ser ˈvir
Con	**la**	**lunghezza**	**del**	**mio**	**servir**
with	the	length	of the	my	serving

With the length of my servitude

la	ˈtu a	fje ˈret: tsa	sa ˈprɔ	staŋ ˈkar
la	**tua**	**fierezza**	**saprò**	**stancar.**
the	your	pride	I will know how	to wear down

I shall wear down your pride.

Sebben, crudele

Anonymous

Antonio Caldara
edited and realized by
Alessandro Parisotti

Come raggio di sol

attributed to
Antonio Caldara
(c1670-1736)

One of the most productive composers of his era, Antonio Caldara began his musical career as a cellist. As a boy Antonio sang in the choir of St. Mark's in his native Venice, and in his musical studies there learned viol, cello and keyboard. Giovanni Legrenzi was *maestro di cappella* at St. Mark's in these years; Caldara was certainly influenced by him. Caldara began publishing works soon after the age of 20, and by 30 was an opera composer. Beginning in 1699, for approximately eight years he was in service to Ferdinando Carlo. After some travels and performances in Spain and time in Rome and other places related to commissions, he settled in Vienna in 1716, where for twenty years until his death he served as vice-Kapellmeister to Emporer Charles VI, a position with a handsome salary which required him to compose over 30 dramatic works.

It is customary to credit Antonio Caldara with "Come raggio di sol," although there is no proof that he composed this aria, nor has any Caldara source been found. Parisotti's source may have been a nineteenth century British collection published in London.

"Come raggio di sol" appeared in Parisotti's *Arie antiche* Volume 1, published by Ricordi in 1885, in the key of E minor. Parisotti's metronomic suggestion was quarter note = 46, a tempo reflecting the romantic age of the edition and significantly slower than is commonly performed today. Parisotti's edition was published by G. Schirmer in 1894 in the *Anthology of Italian Song of the Seventeenth and Eighteenth Centuries*, later included in the 1948 Schirmer compilation *24 Italian Songs and Arias of the Seventeenth and Eighteenth Centuries*.

'ko me	'rad: dʒo	di	sol	'mi te	e	se 're no	'so vra	'pla tʃi di	'flut: ti	si ri 'pɔ za
Come	raggio	di	sol	mite	e	sereno	sovra	placidi	flutti	si riposa,
as	ray	of	sun	mild	and	serene	over	placid	waves	itself reposes

As a ray of sunlight, mild and serene, reposes upon placid waves

'men tre	del	'ma re	nel	pro 'fon do	'se no	sta	la	tem 'pɛ sta	a 'sko za
mentre	del	mare	nel	profondo	seno	sta	la	tempesta	ascosa:
while	of the	sea	in the	profound	breast	is	the	tempest	hidden

while within the deep bosom of the sea lies the hidden tempest,

ko 'zi	'ri zo	ta 'lor	'ga jo	e	pa 'ka to	di	kon 'tɛn to
così	riso	talor	gaio	e	pacato	di	contento,
thus	laughter	at times	cheerful	and	calm	with	contentment

so does laughter, sometimes cheerful and calm with contentment,

di	'dʒɔ ja	un	'lab: bro	in 'fjo ɾa	'men tre	nel	'su o	se 'gre to
di	gioia	un	labbro	infiora,	mentre	nel	suo	segreto
with	joy	a	lip	adorns	while	in the	its	secret

adorn lips with joy while, in its depths,

il	kɔr	pja 'ga to	saŋ 'gɔʃ: ʃa	e	si mar 'tɔ ɾa
il	cor	piagato	s'angoscia	e	si martora.
the	heart	wounded	itself grieves	and	itself tortures

the wounded heart grieves and tortures itself.

Come raggio di sol

attributed to
Antonio Caldara
edited and realized by Alessandro Parisotti

Anonymous

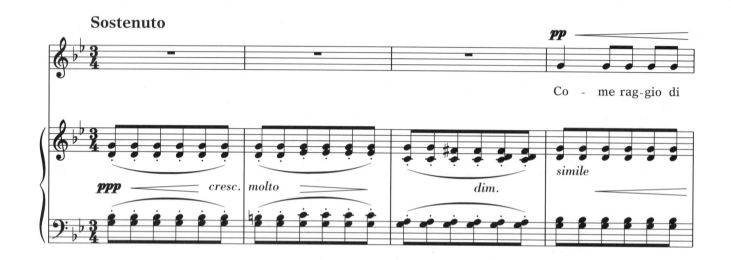

Co - me rag-gio di

sol mi - te e se - re - no, co - me rag-gio di

sol mi - te e se - re - no so - vra

Vittoria, vittoria!

Giacomo Carissimi
(1605-1674)

A singer, organist and priest, the Roman composer Carissimi is most remembered as an influential composer of oratorios. After service as a youth at the Tivoli Cathedral, Carissimi was appointed *maestro di cappella* in 1629 at the leading Jesuit institution of the era, the Collegio Germanico in Rome. He remained there until his death 45 years later, in charge of the education of choirboys and students, and responsible for all music at the church of San Appolinare, associated with the college.

Carissimi remained conventional in his composition of masses and motets, presumably for use in services. However, he was one of the first important and inventive composers of the more freely composed and expressive oratorio, borrowing styles and techniques from opera. During his life he was also known for his secular cantata writing, which was often humorous. "Vittoria, vittoria!" is one of Carissimi's approximately 150 cantatas and its ironic lyrics attest to the composer's wit. Its form of alternating recitative sections with a rhythmic tune was a common cantata device for Carissimi. He was so associated with the solo cantata that many thought he invented it.

Carissimi was so revered that a papal edict prevented the sale of any of his composition manuscripts after his death. When the Jesuit order of Collegio Germanico was dissolved in 1773, however, Carissimi's autographs were lost, an event that seriously hinders research of his works. Except for published works, few manuscript sources survive. Dates are difficult to discern on his compositions.

"Vittoria, vittoria!" was a popular tune, and was published frequently in the seventeenth century. It appeared in Parisotti's *Arie antiche* Volume 1, published by Ricordi in 1885, in the key of C major, with a metronomic suggestion of quarter note = 168. Parisotti's source was *Les gloires d'Italie*, edited by François Aubert Gevaert, published in 1868. The piece was published by G. Schirmer in 1880, also using the Gevaert edition as a source, pre-dating Parisotti's *Arie antiche*. With the title "Vittoria, mio core!" and citing Parisotti as the editor, the song was included in the 1894 Schirmer *Anthology of Italian Song of the Seventeenth and Eighteenth Centuries*, and in the 1948 Schirmer compilation *24 Italian Songs and Arias of the Seventeenth and Eighteenth Centuries*.

vit: 'tɔ ɾja vit: 'tɔ ɾja 'mi o 'kɔ ɾe non la gri 'mar pju
Vittoria! Vittoria, mio core! Non lagrimar più;
victory victory my heart not to weep more
Victory! Victory, my heart! Weep no more;

ɛ 'ʃɔl ta da 'mo ɾe la vil ser vi 'tu ɛ 'ʃɔl ta da 'mo ɾe la ser vi 'tu
è sciolta d'Amore la vil servitù, è sciolta d'Amore la servitù.
is released of Love the vile servitude is released of Love the servitude
the miserable bondage of love is liberated — liberated is the bondage of love.

dʒa 'lem pja a 'twɔ i 'dan: ni fra 'stwɔ lo di 'zgwar di
Già l'empia a' tuoi danni, fra stuolo di sguardi,
formerly the wicked one to your harm among multitude of glances
Formerly the evil woman, to your detriment, among a multitude of glances,

kon 'vet: tsi bu 'dʒar di di 'spɔ ze ʎiŋ 'gan: ni
con vezzi bugiardi dispose gl'inganni.
with charms lying arranged the deceptions
with false charms, planned the deceptions.

le 'frɔ de ʎi af: 'fan: ni non 'an: no pju 'lɔ ko
Le frode, gli affanni non hanno più loco,
the frauds the anxieties not they have more place
The frauds and anxieties exist no more;

del 'kru do 'su o 'fɔ ko ɛ 'spɛn to lar 'do ɾe
del crudo suo foco è spento l'ardore!
of the cruel her fire is extinguished the ardor
the flame of her cruel fire is extinguished!

da 'lu tʃi ri 'dɛn ti non 'ɛʃ: ʃe pju 'stra le
Da luci ridenti non esce più strale,
from eyes smiling not come out more darts
From smiling eyes come no more darts

ke 'pja ga mor 'ta le nel 'pɛt: to mav: 'vɛn ti
che piaga mortale nel petto m'avventi:
which wound mortal in the breast to me you hurl
with which you hurl a mortal wound into my breast:

nel dwɔl ne tor 'men ti 'i o pju non mi 'sfat: tʃo
nel duol, ne' tormenti io più non mi sfaccio;
in the grief in the torments I more not myself I become undone
in grief and torment I no longer become undone;

ɛ 'rot: to 'oɲ: ɲi 'lat: tʃo spa 'ri to il ti 'mo ɾe
è rotto ogni laccio, sparito il timore!
is broken every bond vanished the fear
broken is every bond, vanished is fear!

Vittoria, vittoria!

Domenico Benigni

Giacomo Carissimi
edited and realized by
François Auguste Gevaert
and Alessandro Parisotti

han - no più lo - co, del cru - do suo fo - co è spen - to __ l'ar -

Tempo I

do - re! Vit - to - ria! Vit - to - ria! Vit - to - ria! Vit - to - ria, mio

co - re! Non la - gri - mar più, non la - gri - mar più; è

sciol - ta d'A - mo - re la vil ser - vi - tù, è sciol - - -

Tempo I

ri - to il ti - mo — re! Vit - to - ria! Vit - to - ria! Vit - to - ria! Vit -

to - ria, mio co — re! Non la - gri-mar più, non la - gri-mar

più; è sciol - ta d'A - mo - re la vil ser - vi - tù, è sciol -

ta d'A - mo - re la ser - vi - tù.

Delizie contente
from the opera *Giasone*

Francesco Cavalli
(1602-1676)

Cavalli was the most performed opera composer in Italy after the death of Monteverdi, and succeeded Monteverdi as the leading musical figure of Venice. His birth name was Caletti. He was taken in by Federico Cavalli, Venetian governor of Crema, who persuaded the boy's father to allow him to go back to Venice with him in 1616 at the end of his governorship. Francesco later took the name of his benefactor. Cavalli was a singer in the cathedral choir of St. Mark's in Venice during Monteverdi's time as *maestro di cappella*. He had the opportunity to learn from the older master, and probably was the posthumous editor of some of Monteverdi's music. Due to a financially advantageous marriage in 1630, Cavalli was free to pursue opera composition, though he also became the principal organist at St. Mark's. His first opera, *Le nozze di Teti e di Peleo*, was produced in Venice in 1639. His *Egisto* of 1643 was internationally successful, with productions throughout Italy and Paris. *Giasone* of 1649 was even more successful, one of the two most performed operas of the century (along with Cesti's *Orontea*). These operas were fast paced and comic, breaking tradition with the noble mood of Venetian opera of the 1640s. More operas followed regularly until his last, composed in 1673, with international productions, travel and fame, though his best work was in the 1640s and '50s.

"Delizie contente" is from *Giasone*, first performed in Venice at the public theatre Teatro San Cassiano on January 5, 1649. The opera is a satirical treatment of the Greek myth story of Jason and the Argonauts. Jason obtains the golden fleece and falls in love with Medea, but ultimately returns to Hypsipyle, his first love.

"Delizie contente" appeared in Parisotti's *Arie antiche* Volume 2, published by Ricordi in 1890, in the key of F minor. Parisotti's metronomic suggestion was eighth note = 132, somewhat slower than most performances of today. Parisotti's edition was published in the *Anthology of Italian Song of the Seventeenth and Eighteenth Centuries*, released by G. Schirmer in 1894.

de ˈliːt tsje   kon ˈtɛn te   ke   ˈlal ma   be ˈa te   fer ˈma te
Delizie   **contente**   **che**   **l'alma**   **beate,**   **fermate.**
delights   pleasing   that   the soul   you make happy   stop
Pleasing delights, you who make the soul happy, cease.

su   ˈkwe sto   ˈmi o   ˈkɔ ɾe   dɛ   pju   non   stilː ˈla te   le   ˈdʒɔ je   da ˈmo ɾe
Su   **questo**   **mio**   **core**   **deh**   **più**   **non**   **stillate**   **le**   **gioie**   **d'amore.**
on   this   my   heart   ah   more   not   drip   the   joys   of love
Ah, upon this heart of mine no longer trickle the joys of love.

de ˈliːt tsje   ˈmi e   ˈka ɾe   fer ˈma te vi   kwi
Delizie   **mie**   **care,**   **fermatevi**   **qui:**
delights   mine   dear   stop you   here
My dear delights, stop here:

non   sɔ   pju   bra ˈma ɾe   mi   ˈba sta   ko ˈzi
non   **so**   **più**   **bramare,**   **mi**   **basta**   **così.**
not   I know how   more   to desire   to me   is enough   like this
I know not how to desire anymore; this is enough for me.

in   ˈgrɛm bo   ˈaʎː ʎi   a ˈmo ɾi   fra   ˈdol tʃi   ka ˈte ne   mo ˈrir   mi   kon ˈvje ne
In   **grembo**   **agli**   **amori**   **fra**   **dolci**   **catene,**   **morir**   **mi**   **conviene.**
in   lap   of the   loves   among   sweet   chains   to die   to me   is better
In the lap of love, among sweet chains, it is better for me to die.

dol ˈtʃet tsa   o mi ˈtʃi da   a   ˈmɔr te   mi   ˈgwi da   in   ˈbratː tʃo   al   ˈmi o   ˈbɛ ne
Dolcezza   **omicida,**   **a**   **morte**   **mi**   **guida**   **in**   **braccio**   **al**   **mio**   **bene.**
sweetness   murderous   to   death   me   guide   into   arm   to the   my   dear one
Murderous sweetness, lead me to death in the arms of my dear one.

dol ˈtʃet tse   ˈmi e   ˈka ɾe   fer ˈma te vi   kwi   non   sɔ   pju   bra ˈma ɾe
Dolcezze   **mie**   **care,**   **fermatevi**   **qui:**   **non**   **so**   **più**   **bramare...**
sweetnesses   mine   dear   stop you   here   not   I know how   more   to desire
My dear sweetnesses, stop here: I know not how to desire anymore...

Delizie contente

Giacinto Andrea Cicognini

Francesco Cavalli
edited and realized by
Alessandro Parisotti

Andantino mosso

De - li - zie con - ten - te che l'al - ma be - a - te,

fer - ma - te,

fer - ma - te. Su que - sto mio

ca - re,   fer - ma - te - vi qui:

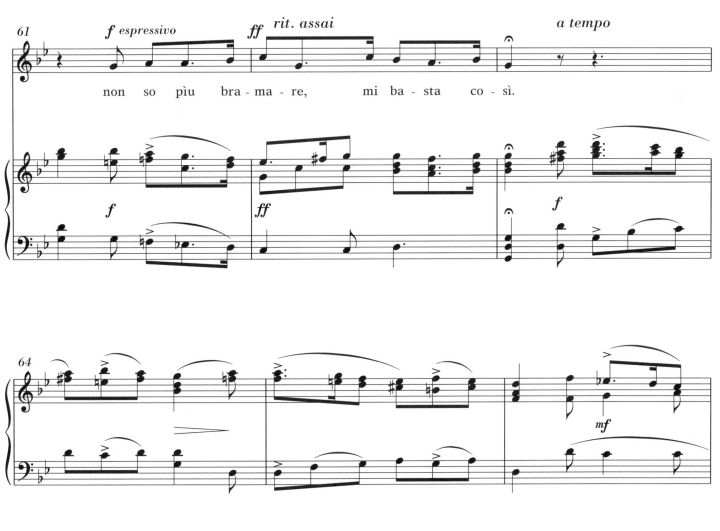

non so più bra - ma - re,   mi ba - sta co - sì.

Danza, danza

Francesco Durante
(1684-1755)

Durante was trained in Naples by his uncle, head of the San Onofrio a Capuana conservatory. From 1705 on he undoubtedly studied and composed, and must have achieved some degree of notoriety and accomplishment, but there is little known of him until 1728 when Durante was appointed head of the Poveri di Gesù Cristo conservatory in Naples. His compositions from this period, ranging from masses and sacred dramas to instrumental and keyboard works, are easier to date. In his 11 years at the conservatory he had great influence as a teacher, with Pergolesi as one of his students. In 1742 he became head of the Santa Maria di Loreto conservatory in Naples, the most prestigious musical position in the city.

Durante composed a large number of pedagogical pieces. Like "Vergin, tutt'amor," "Danza, danza" first appeared in one of Durante's solfeggio collections for voice students, without words. The song appeared with text over a century later in Lorenzo Pagans' *Échos d'Italie*. No credit was given for the authorship of the text.

"Danza, danza" appeared in Parisotti's *Arie antiche* Volume 2, published by Ricordi in 1890, in the key of B-flat minor, with a metronomic suggestion of quarter note = 138. With the extended title "Danza, danza, fanciulla gentile" Parisotti's edition was published by G. Schirmer in 1894 in the *Anthology of Italian Song of the Seventeenth and Eighteenth Centuries (Volume II)*, later included in the 1948 Schirmer compilation *24 Italian Songs and Arias of the Seventeenth and Eighteenth Centuries*.

ˈdan tsa ˈdan tsa fan ˈtʃul: la al   ˈmi o kan ˈtar
Danza, **danza,** **fanciulla,** **al**   **mio** **cantar;**
dance   dance   maiden   to the my singing
Dance, dance, maiden, to my singing;

ˈdan tsa ˈdan tsa fan ˈtʃul: la dʒen ˈti le al   ˈmi o kan ˈtar
Danza, **danza,** **fanciulla** **gentile,** **al**   **mio** **cantar.**
dance   dance   maiden   gentle   to the my singing
dance, dance, gentle maiden, to my singing.

ˈdʒi ɾa led: ˈdʒɛ ɾa sot: ˈti le al   ˈswɔ no del: ˈlon de del   mar
Gira **leggera,** **sottile** **al**   **suono** **dell'onde** **del**   **mar.**
whirl   light   slender   to the sound   of the waves of the sea
Whirl, light and slender girl, to the sound of the waves of the sea.

ˈsɛn ti il   ˈva ɡo ru ˈmo ɾe del: ˈla u ɾa sker ˈtso za
Senti **il**   **vago** **rumore** **dell'aura** **scherzosa**
hear   the   pleasant noise   of the breeze playful
Hear the pleasant murmur of the playful breeze

ke   ˈpar la al   ˈkɔ ɾe kon ˈlaŋ ɡwi do swɔn
che   **parla** **al**   **core** **con** **languido** **suon,**
which speaks to the heart with languid   sound
which speaks to the heart with languid voice

e   ke   in ˈvi ta a   dan ˈtsar ˈsɛn tsa ˈpɔ za
e   **che**   **invita** **a**   **danzar** **senza** **posa.**
and   which invites to   to dance without repose
and which invites dancing without rest.

ˈdan tsa ˈdan tsa fan ˈtʃul: la dʒen ˈti le al   ˈmi o kan ˈta ɾe
Danza, **danza,** **fanciulla** **gentile,** **al**   **mio** **cantare.**
dance   dance   maiden   gentle   to the my singing
Dance, dance, gentle maiden, to my singing.

Danza, danza

Anonymous

Francesco Durante
edited and realized by
Lorenzo Pagans and
Alessandro Parisotti

Allegro con spirito

Dan - za, — dan - za, fan - ciul - la, — al — mi - o can -
tar; Dan - za, — dan - za, — fan - ciul - la — gen - ti - le, al
mi - o can - tar. Gi - ra leg - ge - ra, sot -

Vergin, tutt'amor

Francesco Durante
(1684-1755)

Durante was trained in Naples by his uncle, head of the San Onofrio a Capuana conservatory. From 1705 on he undoubtedly studied and composed, and must have achieved some degree of notoriety and accomplishment, but there is little known of him until 1728 when Durante was appointed head of the Poveri di Gesù Cristo conservatory in Naples. His compositions from this period, ranging from masses and sacred dramas to instrumental and keyboard works, are easier to date. In his 11 years at the conservatory he had great influence as a teacher, with Pergolesi as one of his students. In 1742 he became head of the Santa Maria di Loreto conservatory in Naples, the most prestigious musical position in the city.

Durante composed a large number of pedagogical pieces. Like "Danza, danza," "Vergin, tutt'amor" first appeared in one of Durante's solfeggio collections for voice students, without words. The song appeared with text over a century later in Lorenzo Pagans' *Échos d'Italie*. No credit was given for the authorship of the text.

"Vergin, tutt'amor" appeared in Parisotti's *Arie antiche* Volume 2, published by Ricordi in 1890, in the key of C minor. Parisotti's metronomic suggestion was dotted quarter note = 40, a tempo reflecting the romantic age of the edition and slower than is commonly performed today. Parisotti's edition was published by G. Schirmer in 1894 in the *Anthology of Italian Song of the Seventeenth and Eighteenth Centuries (Volume II)*, later included in the 1948 Schirmer compilation *24 Italian Songs and Arias of the Seventeenth and Eighteenth Centuries*.

Note that the title and first words used in the previously published Schirmer editions, "Vergin tutto amor," have been corrected to "Vergin tutt'amor." In Parisotti's edition "Vergin tutt'amor" appears as the title, though "Vergin, tutto amor" appears in the musical score, possibly an oversight.

'ver dʒin   'tut: ta 'mor   o   'ma dre   di   bon 'ta de   o   'ma dre   'pi a
Vergin,   **tutt'amor,**   **o**   **madre**   **di**   **bontade,**   **o**   **madre**   **pia,**
virgin   all love   o   mother   of   goodness   o   mother   pious
Virgin, absolute love, o mother of goodness, o pious mother,

a 'skol ta   'dol tʃe   ma 'ri a   la   'vo tʃe   del   pek: ka 'tor
ascolta,   **dolce**   **Maria,**   **la**   **voce**   **del**   **peccator.**
listen to   sweet   Mary   the   voice   of the   sinner
listen, sweet Mary, to the voice of the sinner.

il   'pjan to   'su o   ti   'mwɔ va   'dʒuŋ ga no   a   te   i   'swɔ i   la 'men ti
Il   **pianto**   **suo**   **ti**   **muova,**   **giungano**   **a**   **te**   **i**   **suoi**   **lamenti,**
the   weeping   his   you   let move   let reach   to   you   the   his   laments
May his weeping move you, may his laments reach you;

'su o   dwɔl   'swɔ i   'tri sti   at: 'tʃen ti   'sɛn ti   pje 'to zo   kwel   'tu o   kɔr
suo   **duol,**   **suoi**   **tristi**   **accenti,**   **senti**   **pietoso**   **quel**   **tuo**   **cor.**
his   grief   his   sad   words   let hear   with pity   that   your   heart
may that compassionate heart of yours hear his grief, his sad words.

o   'ma dre   di   bon 'ta de   'ver dʒin   'tut: ta 'mor
O   **madre**   **di**   **bontade,**   **Vergin,**   **tutt'amor.**
o   mother   of   goodness   virgin   all love
O mother of goodness, virgin, absolute love.

Vergin, tutt'amor

Anonymous

Francesco Durante
edited and realized by
Lorenzo Pagans and
Alessandro Parisotti

Largo religioso

Ver - gin, tut - t'a - mor, o ma - dre di bon - ta - de, o ma - dre pi - a, ma - dre pi - a, a - scol - ta, dol - ce Ma - ri - a, la _____ vo - ce del pec - ca -

Intorno all'idol mio
from the opera *Orontea*

Antonio Cesti
(1623-1669)

Antonio Cesti was one of the most celebrated mid-seventeenth century Italian opera composers. Though he did not spend a great deal of time in Venice, his style is typically Venetian, in the same style as Cavalli. Pietro (Cesti's birth name) served as a choirboy in Arezzo, taking the name Antonio upon joining the Franciscan order in 1637. His life as a priest often came in conflict with his life as a composer. He was rebuked on numerous occasions by his order in Arezzo for his "dishonorable and irregular life." Cesti is said to have written over 100 operas, but only 15 of these scores survived. The most prominent are *Orontea* (1649), *La Dori* (1661), and *Il pomo d'oro* (1667). Unlike the adventurous chromaticism of Monteverdi or Cavalli, Cesti's music rarely strays from simple harmonic progressions. It instead relies on smoother contours and regular, often sequential patterns, rarely stressing rhythmic play.

Orontea was Cesti's first opera, produced in Venice in 1649. It was revised by librettist Giovanni Filippo Apolloni for an Innsbruck production of 1656, and grew in international reputation and popularity to become one of the two most produced of seventeenth century operas (the other being Cavalli's *Giasone*), showing a taste for fast paced comedy. *Orontea*, queen of Egypt, falls in love with Alidoro, a painter and a commoner who is also pursued by another lady, who is herself pursued by Corindo. Misunderstandings mount, but the queen's wedding hopes are realized when Alidoro is revealed actually to be a Phoenician prince.

"Intorno all'idol mio" appeared in Parisotti's *Arie antiche* Volume 1, published by Ricordi in 1885, in the key of E minor. Parisotti's metronomic suggestion was quarter note = 84. Parisotti's source, which he cited, was *Arien und Gesänge ältere Tonmeister*, edited by Carl Banck and published in 1880. The same edition was published in the *Anthology of Italian Song of the Seventeenth and Eighteenth Centuries*, released by G. Schirmer in 1894.

in 'tor no	al: 'li dol	'mi o	spi 'ra te	pur	spi 'ra te	'a u re	so 'a vi	e	'gra te
Intorno	all'idol	mio	spirate	pur,	spirate,	aure	soavi	e	grate;
around	to the idol	mine	blow	then	blow	breezes	gentle	and	pleasant

Blow, gentle and pleasant breezes, around my idol;

e	'nel: le	'gwan tʃe	e 'lɛt: te	ba 'tʃa te lo	per	me	kor 'te zi	a u 'ret: te
e	nelle	guancie	elette	baciatelo	per	me,	cortesi	aurette!
and	on the	cheeks	chosen	kiss him	for	me	kind	little breezes

and kiss his precious cheeks for me, kind little breezes!

al	'mi o	bɛn	ke	ri 'pɔ za	su	'la li	'del: la	'kwjɛ te
Al	mio	ben,	che	riposa	su	l'ali	della	quiete,
to the	my	dear one	who	sleeps	on	the wings	of the	repose

'gra ti	'soɲ: ɲi	as: si 'ste te
grati	sogni	assistete,
pleasant	dreams	aid

Aid my dear one, who sleeps on the wings of repose, with pleasant dreams,

e	il	'mi o	rak: 'kju zo	ar 'do ɾe	zve 'la te ʎi	per	me	o	'lar ve	da 'mo ɾe
e	il	mio	racchiuso	ardore	svelategli	per	me,	o	larve	d'amore!
and	the	my	enclosed	ardor	reveal to him	for	me	o	shadows	of love

and reveal to him for me my inner ardor, o spirits of love!

Intorno all'idol mio

Giacinto Andrea Cicognini

Antonio Cesti
edited and realized by
Alessandro Parisotti

Caro mio ben

assumably by
Tommaso Giordani
(1730 or 33-1806)

The authorship of "Caro mio ben" has long been a source of controversy. The song was first published in London in the late eighteenth century with the composer credit "Signor Giordani." Parisotti's *Arie antiche* credits Giuseppe Giordani (c1753-1798) with "Caro mio ben." Tommaso Giordani has also been credited as the composer elsewhere. Though unrelated, they were both born in Naples and both wrote operas, but led different careers. In its article on Giuseppe Giordani *Grove Dictionary of Music and Musicians* states that "works published in London and Paris under the name of 'Signor Giordani' may safely be credited to Tommaso, who was sufficiently popular to dispense with a first name." Contradictory to that, the same source's article on Tommaso Giordani states, "It seems likely that the popular song 'Caro mio ben' often attributed to him was actually by Giuseppe Giordani."

There is not enough evidence to firmly determine which "Signor Giordani" actually composed "Caro mio ben," which has remained famous for more than 200 years. But it is likely that Tommaso Giordani is the composer, since the song was first performed in London during a time of his activity there.

Tommaso Giordani traveled Europe with an opera company comprised primarily of family members, arriving in England in 1753. Records show his first London opera production as being in 1756. He created operas for London and Dublin through the 1760s until 1783, when he settled in Dublin. Giordani wrote instrumental works, sacred works, and taught pupils when income demanded it. His critics often accused him of plagiarism.

Giuseppe Giordani was a student at the Conservatorio Santa Maria along with Cimarosa and Zingarelli. His 30 operas were produced in Florence, Naples, Rome, Bergamo and other Italian cities. He was *maestro di cappella* for the last seven years of his life at Fermo Cathedral.

"Caro mio ben" appeared in Parisotti's *Arie antiche* Volume 2, published by Ricordi in 1890, in the key of E-flat major. Parisotti's metronomic suggestion was quarter note = 60. Parisotti's edition was published by G. Schirmer in 1894 in the *Anthology of Italian Song of the Seventeenth and Eighteenth Centuries*, later included in the 1948 Schirmer compilation *24 Italian Songs and Arias of the Seventeenth and Eighteenth Centuries*.

'ka ɾo	'mi o	'bɛn	'kre di mi	al 'men	'sɛn tsa	di	te	laŋ 'gwi ʃe	il	kɔr
Caro	mio	ben,	credimi	almen,	senza	di	te	languisce	il	cor.
dear	my	beloved	believe me	at least	without	of	you	languishes	the	heart

My dear beloved one, believe me at least: without you my heart languishes.

il	'tu o	fe 'del	so 'spi ɾa	oɲ 'ɲor	'tʃɛs: sa	kru 'dɛl	'tan to	ri 'gor
Il	tuo	fedel	sospira	ognor.	Cessa,	crudel,	tanto	rigor!
the	your	faithful one	sighs	always	cease	cruel one	so much	severity

Your faithful one yearns for you always. Stop being so stern with me, cruel one!

Caro mio ben

Anonymous

assumably by
Tommaso Giordani
edited by
Alessandro Parisotti

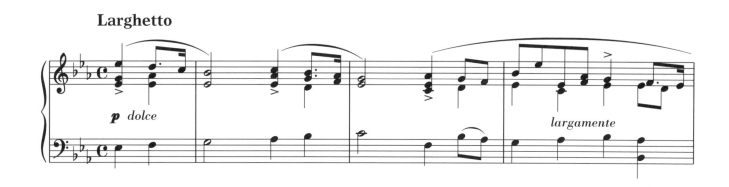

cor.   Il tuo fe - del   so - spi - ra o -

gnor.   Ces - sa, cru - del, __ tan - to ri - gor!   Ces - sa, cru -

del,   tan - to ri - gor, __ tan - to ri - gor!   Ca - ro mio

ben, cre - di - mi al-men, sen - za di te ___ lan - gui - sce il

cor, ca - ro mio ben, cre - di - mi al-men, sen - za di

te ___ lan - gui - sce il cor.

O del mio dolce ardor
from the opera *Paride ed Elena*

Christoph Willibald von Gluck
(1714-1787)

Gluck was one of the most important opera composers in history, known as the "second founder of opera" for his progressive development of the modern music-drama, moving away from Baroque models. He was born in Germany and raised in northern Bohemia by a strict father who discouraged a pursuit of music. By 14 Gluck moved to Prague where he found an incomplete formal education, but immersed himself in the music making of the city, also working as an organist. He moved to Vienna by 1735, and after two years there was engaged by a nobleman for his orchestra in Milan, where he was mentored by Sammartini, evident in Gluck's compositions of the period. His first opera was produced in Milan in 1741. The composer found immediate success and Italian commissions soon followed. Gluck moved to London in 1745, where he met and worked with Handel, who was dismayed with Gluck's lack of contrapuntal skill as a composer. It may have been a fair observation, but this was also perhaps an older composer's Baroque style expectations. Gluck traveled internationally following commissions, settling in Vienna in 1752 in service to the court. He also composed operas for Paris in his years in Vienna.

Partnering with librettist Calzabigi on *Orfeo ed Euridice* (1762) began Gluck's process of more closely aligning music and drama. By his opera *Alceste* (1767) the composer's ideas about the future of opera had become clear. In the preface to *Alceste* Gluck listed the goals of his reform: simplicity and tonal clarity, an end to the excesses and abuses of singers, and the restriction of music "to its true office by means of expression and by following the situation of the story." Opera at this time had become highly stylized and stale in its predictable, formal plots and structure, with superfluous musical numbers having little connection to the plot or characters, and singers profusely ornamenting melodies to distortion. Gluck's ideas met with enthusiasm and controversy for years to come in Vienna and Paris.

"O del mio dolce ardor" comes from Gluck's five-act opera *Paride ed Elena* (Paris and Helen) with a libretto by Calzabigi, the third of his reform operas after *Alceste*. *Paride ed Elena* was first performed in Vienna on November 3, 1770. In ancient Greece Paris pursues Helen, who at first dismisses him. Through the help of Erasto (actually Cupid in disguise), Helen gives way to Paris, and the couple embarks for Troy. This aria from Act I is sung by Paris, a prince of Troy, as a declaration of love for Helen. The role of Paris was written for a castrato; in modern times the role has been adapted for tenor, soprano and mezzo-soprano.

"O del mio dolce ardor" appeared in Parisotti's *Arie antiche* Volume 1, published by Ricordi in 1885, in the key of E minor. Parisotti's metronomic suggestion was quarter note = 46, a tempo reflecting the romantic age of the edition and significantly slower than is commonly performed today. Parisotti's cited source was *Les gloires de l'Italie*, edited by François Auguste Gevaert, published in Paris, 1868. Parisotti's edition of the aria was published by G. Schirmer in 1894 in the *Anthology of Italian Song of the Seventeenth and Eighteenth Centuries*, later included in the 1948 Schirmer compilation *24 Italian Songs and Arias of the Seventeenth and Eighteenth Centuries*.

o   del   ˈmi o   ˈdol tʃe   ar ˈdor   bra ˈma to   od ˈdʒɛtː to
O   del   mio   dolce   ardor   bramato   oggetto,
o   of the   my   sweet   ardor   longed for   object
O desired object of my sweet ardor,

ˈla u ɾa   ke   tu   re ˈspi ɾi   al ˈfin   re ˈspi ɾo
l'aura   che   tu   respiri,   alfin   respiro.
the air   which   you   breathe   at last   I breathe
at last I breathe the air which you breathe.

o ˈvuŋ kwe   il   ˈgwar do   ˈi o   ˈdʒi ɾo
Ovunque   il   guardo   io   giro,
wherever   the   glance   I   I turn
Wherever I turn my glance,

le   ˈtu e   ˈva ge   sem ˈbjan tse   a ˈmo ɾe   in   me   di ˈpin dʒe
le   tue   vaghe   sembianze   amore   in   me   dipinge:
the   your   lovely   features   love   in   me   depicts
love depicts to me your beautiful image:

il   ˈmi o   pen ˈsjɛr   si   ˈfin dʒe   le   pju   ˈljɛ te   spe ˈran tse
il   mio   pensier   si   finge   le   più   liete   speranze;
the   my   thought   to itself   imagines   the   most   happy   hopes
my thoughts imagine the most happy hopes;

e   nel   de ˈzi o   ke   ko ˈzi   ˈmem pje   il   ˈpɛtː to
e   nel   desio   che   così   m'empie   il   petto
and   in the   desire   which   thus   me fills   the   breast
and in the desire which thus fills my breast

ˈtʃer ko   te   ˈkja mo   te   ˈspɛ ɾo   e   so ˈspi ɾo   a
cerco   te,   chiamo   te,   spero   e   sospiro.   Ah!
I search for   you   I call   you   I hope   and   I sigh   Ah
I search for you, I call to you, I hope and I sigh. Ah!

O del mio dolce ardor

Raniero de Calzabigi

Christoph Willibald von Gluck
edited by François Auguste Gevaert
and Alessandro Parisotti

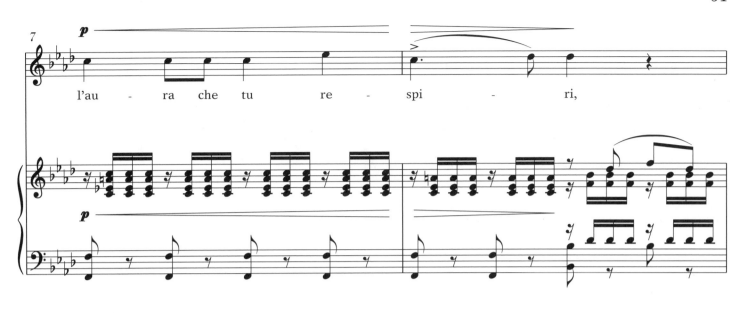

l'au - ra che tu re - spi - ri,

al - fin re - spi - ro,

al - fin ___ re - spi -

O del mio dol - ce ar - dor _____ bra -

ma - to og-get - to, bra - ma - to og -

get - to, l'au - ra che tu re -

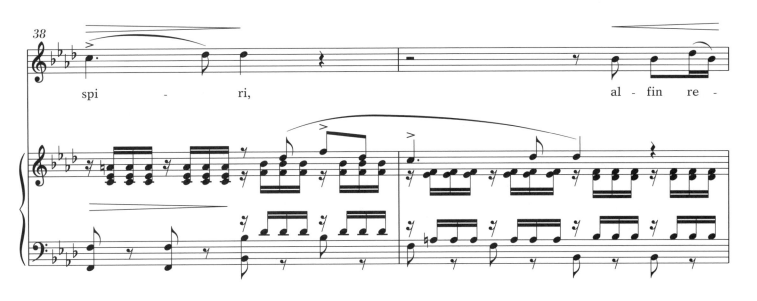

spi - ri, al fin re -

spi - ro, al -

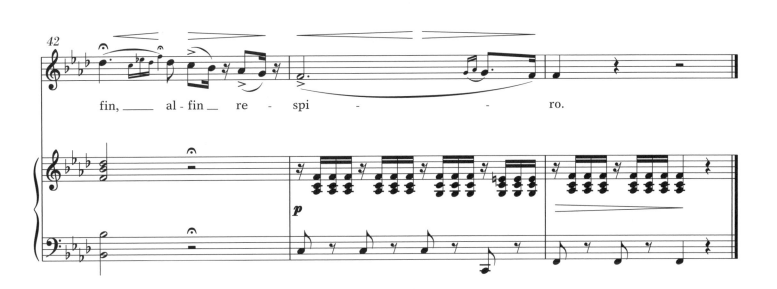

fin,___ al - fin___ re - spi - ro.

Che fiero costume
from the cantata *Echi di riverenza*

Giovanni Legrenzi
(1626-1690)

Legrenzi was one of the most important and influential composers during the last decades of the eighteenth century in the development of a northern Italian late Baroque style, stressing clarity of harmony and rhythm. His humble beginnings were as the son of a violinist and minor composer. Legrenzi was first an organist, and in 1656 became *maestro di cappella* of the Accademia dello Spirito Santo in Ferrara, which was dedicated to the preservation and performance of sacred music. In his decade in Ferrara he composed primarily church music, although he wrote three operas in this period. His career is not clear in the next 12 years; he published only church music in this period. He sought high court positions in Vienna and Versailles, but did not achieve them. By 1671 Legrenzi was teaching at the Conservatorio dei Mendicanti in Venice, and in 1675 began composing operas and oratorios again. He obtained other appointments in Venice, eventually as vice-maestro of St. Mark's. Some of Legrenzi's earlier operas contained more than 90 arias, with later operas pared to down to contain approximately 60 arias. Many of his operas incorporated special effects and spectacles such as fires or storms.

"Che fiero costume" comes from the cantata *Echi di riverenza*, published in Bologna in 1678, reproduced in facsimile by Garland Press in *The Italian Cantata* volume 6. The cantata included recitative and another aria.

"Che fiero costume" appeared in Parisotti's *Arie antiche* Volume 1, published by Ricordi in 1885, in the key of G minor. Parisotti's source was *Arien und Gesänge ältere Tonmeister*, edited by Carl Banck and published in 1880. Parisotti's metronomic suggestion was dotted quarter note = 56, a tempo reflecting the romantic age of the edition and generally slower than is commonly performed today. The Parisotti edition was published by G. Schirmer in 1894 in the *Anthology of Italian Song of the Seventeenth and Eighteenth Centuries*, later included in the 1948 Schirmer compilation *24 Italian Songs and Arias of the Seventeenth and Eighteenth Centuries*.

ke	ˈfjɛ ɾo	ko ˈstu me	da ˈli dʒe ɾo	ˈnu me
Che	fiero	costume	d'aligero	nume,
what	cruel	habit	of winged	deity

What a cruel habit of the winged deity,

ke	a ˈfɔr tsa di	ˈpe ne	si ˈfat: tʃa	a do ˈɾar
che	a forza di	pene	si faccia	adorar!
that	through	sufferings	himself he makes	to adore

that through suffering he makes us adore him!

e	pur	nel: lar ˈdo ɾe	il	ˈdi o	tra di ˈto ɾe
E	pur	nell'ardore	il	dio	traditore
and	yet	in the passion	the	god	treacherous

And yet, in passion, the treacherous god

un	ˈva go	sem ˈbjan te	mi	fe	i do la ˈtrar
un	vago	sembiante	mi	fe'	idolatrar.
a	lovely	countenance	me	made	to idolize

made me idolize a lovely face.

ke	ˈkru do	de ˈsti no	ke	un	ˈtʃɛ ko	bam ˈbi no
Che	crudo	destino	che	un	cieco	bambino
what	cruel	destiny	that	a	blind	child

What a cruel fate, that a blind child,

kon	ˈbok: ka	di	ˈlat: te	si ˈfat: tʃa	sti ˈmar
con	bocca	di	latte	si faccia	stimar!
with	mouth	of	milk	himself he makes	to esteem

barely weaned, makes himself esteemed!

ma	ˈkwe sto	ti ˈran: no	kon	ˈbar ba ɾo	iŋ ˈgan: no
Ma	questo	tiranno	con	barbaro	inganno,
but	this	tyrant	with	barbarous	deception

But this tyrant, with barbarous deception,

en ˈtran do	per	ʎi	ˈɔk: ki	mi	fe	so spi ˈɾar
entrando	per	gli	occhi,	mi	fe'	sospirar.
entering	through	the	eyes	me	he made	to sigh

entering through my eyes, made me sigh.

Che fiero costume

Anonymous

Giovanni Legrenzi
edited and realized by
Carl Banck and
Alessandro Parisotti

un poco meno mosso

E pur nell'-ar-do-re il dio tra-di-to-re un

espress.

va - go sem-bian-te mi fe' i-do - la-trar, _____ un va - go sem-bian-te mi

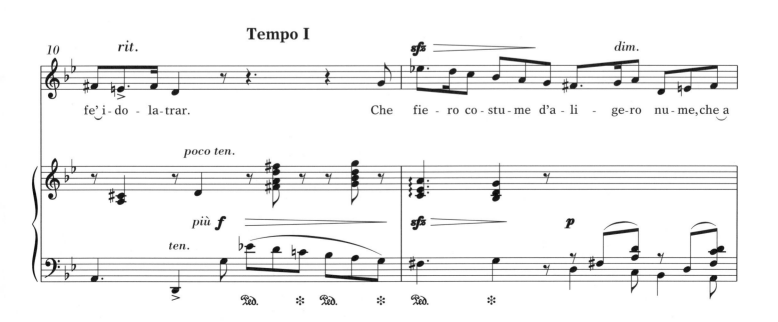

Tempo I

rit.

fe' i-do - la-trar. Che fie - ro co-stu-me d'a - li - ge-ro nu-me, che a

for - za di pe - ne si fac-cia a - do-rar, si fac-cia a - do-rar, _____ che a

for - za di pe - ne si fac-cia a - do-rar!

Che cru - do de - sti - no che un cie - co bam - bi - no con

boc - ca di lat - te si fac - cia sti-mar, si fac - cia sti-mar, _____ con

boc - ca di lat - te si fac - cia sti-mar! _____

un poco meno mosso

Ma que-sto ti - ran - no con bar - ba-ro in-gan - no, en -

Pur dicesti, o bocca bella

Antonio Lotti
(c1667-1740)

Lotti's father was Kapellmeister in Hanover, where Antonio may have been born. By the age of 16 Lotti was studying with Legrenzi in Venice, where he was an organist at St. Mark's from 1692 until his appointment as *maestro di cappella* in 1736. Lotti was also an important teacher whose students included Benedetto Marcello, composer of "Quella fiamma che m'accende," and Giuseppe Saratelli. Besides writing a great deal of sacred music for St. Mark's, Lotti composed duets, madrigals, secular cantatas, motets, masses, oratorios, psalms and instrumental pieces. His operas were regularly produced in Venice, particularly between 1706 and 1717. Lotti's music is noted for creative counterpoint. His compositions for voice and chorus are marked by naturally flowing vocal lines. The origin of "Pur dicesti, o bocca bella" is not known. It is probably from an opera or a secular cantata.

"Pur dicesti, o bocca bella" appeared in Parisotti's *Arie antiche* Volume 1, published by Ricordi in 1885, in the key of D major. Parisotti's source was François Auguste Gevaert's edition *Les glories de l'Italie*, published in Paris, 1868, which Parisotti re-edited. Parisotti's metronomic suggestion was quarter note = 69, a tempo reflecting the romantic age of the edition and significantly slower than is commonly performed today. The Parisotti edition was published by G. Schirmer in 1894 in the *Anthology of Italian Song of the Seventeenth and Eighteenth Centuries*, later included in the 1948 Schirmer compilation *24 Italian Songs and Arias of the Seventeenth and Eighteenth Centuries*.

pur	di ˈtʃe sti	o	ˈbok: ka	ˈbɛl: la	kwel	so ˈa ve	e	ˈka ɾo	si
Pur	**dicesti,**	**o**	**bocca**	**bella,**	**quel**	**soave**	**e**	**caro**	**sì,**
indeed	you said	o	mouth	beautiful	that	sweet	and	dear	yes

Indeed you said, o beautiful mouth, that sweet and dear "yes"

ke	fa	ˈtut: to	il	ˈmi o	pja ˈtʃer
che	**fa**	**tutto**	**il**	**mio**	**piacer.**
which	makes	all	the	my	pleasure

which causes all my pleasure.

per	o ˈnor	di	ˈsu a	fa ˈtʃɛl: la	kon	un	ˈba tʃo	a ˈmor	ta ˈpri
Per	**onor**	**di**	**sua**	**facella**	**con**	**un**	**bacio**	**Amor**	**t'aprì,**
for	honor	of	his	flame	with	a	kiss	Love	you opened

In honor of his flame, Love opened you with a kiss,

ˈdol tʃe	ˈfon te	del	go ˈder	a	si	del	go ˈder
dolce	**fonte**	**del**	**goder,**	**ah!**	**sì,**	**del**	**goder.**
sweet	fount	of the	pleasure	ah	yes	of the	pleasure

sweet fount of pleasure — ah, yes, of pleasure.

Pur dicesti, o bocca bella

Anonymous

Antonio Lotti
edited and realized by
François Auguste Gevaert
and Alessandro Parisotti

*These vocal ornaments were in Parisotti's edition.

sì, che fa tut - to il mio pia - cer, il

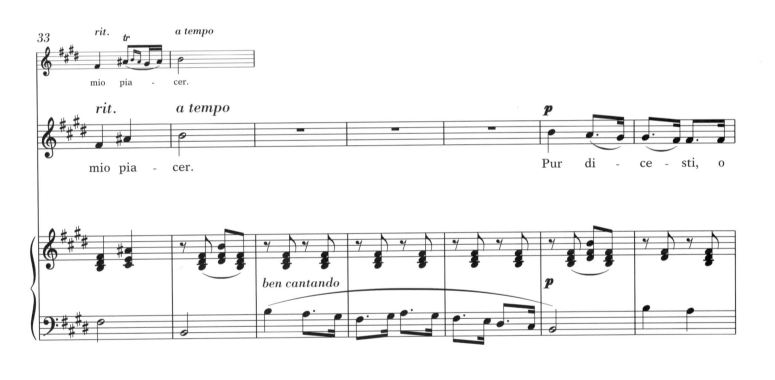

mio pia - cer. mio pia - cer. Pur di - ce - sti, o

boc - ca, boc - ca bel - la, o boc - ca, boc - ca bel - la, quel so - a - ve e

sì, sì, che __ fa tut - to il mio pia - cer, _____

mio pia - cer.

il mio pia - cer.

ben cantando

Fine

Per o - nor di sua fa - cel - la con __ un __ ba - cio A - mor t'a -

D.S. al Fine

Lasciatemi morire!
from the opera *Arianna*

Claudio Monteverdi
(1567-1643)

Claudio Monteverdi was one of the most influential composers in the history of music, a transitional figure from the Renaissance to the Baroque. He was a master composer of madrigals and sacred works, and the first great opera composer. Though he was not necessarily the trailblazing inventor of new genres and forms, they blossomed as a result of his creative genius. Monteverdi infused his works with a deep understanding of humanity and psychology, creating natural drama. He grew up in Cremona, southeast of Milan and north of Parma, the son of a chemist-physician of modest means. Claudio's mother died before he was nine years old. His stepmother died by the time he was 16, and his father married a third time. Claudio studied in private lessons with the maestro of the local cathedral and even at a young age published motets in 1582, sacred madrigals in 1583, and canzonettas in 1584. Monteverdi was a musician (he played both the viola da gamba and viola da braccio, or violin) and composer in service at the court of Duke Vincenzo I of Mantua by 1592. Monteverdi was well-known as a composer as the new century began; he was made *maestro di cappella* at Mantua in 1601. His important fourth and fifth books of madrigals were published in 1603 and 1605.

Following trends of the day, Monteverdi turned his attention to opera and the musical style of monody. His *Orfeo* was produced for the Accademia degli Invaghiti in Mantua in February of 1607, the first work to indicate the potential of the then infant genre of opera. A second opera, *L'Arianna*, commissioned as part of the wedding celebrations of the Duke of Mantua's son, was first produced on May 28, 1608, and with great success. It is quite possible that the sad power of the lament from this opera, "Lasciatemi morire!," was influenced by the death of Monteverdi's wife in September of the previous year. Unhappy in Mantua under the reign of Duke Francesco, Monteverdi became *maestro di cappella* at St. Mark's in Venice in 1612. Though he was busy with duties at the Venetian cathedral, he composed and published for the rest of his life, with operas and ballets as occasional but conspicuous pursuits among his composition of many secular and sacred vocal works. His last burst of operatic activity came after the opening of the public opera houses in Venice in 1637, including a revival of *L'Arianna* in 1640, and three operas from 1640 to 1642: *Il ritorno d'Ulisse in patria*, *Le nozze d'Enea con Lavinia*, and *L'incoronazione di Poppea*.

In *L'Arianna*, based on Greek myth, Ariadne (Arianna) sings "Lasciatemi morire!" when realizing that she has been abandoned on the island of Naxos by her lover, Theseus, whose escape she had aided from the Labyrinth of the Minotaur. Dionysus, the Greek god of wine, discovers Ariadne and weds her. This lament is the only surviving section of the opera. The extended scene is longer than the excerpt that appears in Parisotti's edition. The lament was immensely popular in the seventeenth century. It was published separately in 1623, insuring its later survival. Monteverdi created a five-part madrigal version of it in 1614, and later used the music as a sacred contrafactum in *Pianto della Madonna* from the *Selva Morale e Spirituale*. Other composers made arrangements for various instrumentations, including keyboard.

"Lasciatemi morire!" appeared in Parisotti's *Arie antiche* Volume 2, published by Ricordi in 1890, in the key of F minor. Parisotti's metronomic suggestion was quarter note = 58. Parisotti's edition was published by G. Schirmer in 1894 in the *Anthology of Italian Song of the Seventeenth and Eighteenth Centuries (Book II)*, later included in the 1948 Schirmer compilation *24 Italian Songs and Arias of the Seventeenth and Eighteenth Centuries*.

laʃ: 'ʃa te mi   mo 'ri ɾe   e   ke   vo 'le te   ke   mi   kon 'fɔr te
Lasciatemi   morire!   E   che   volete   che   mi   conforte
leave me   to die   and   what   you want   that   me   it should comfort
Let me die! What would you have comfort me

iŋ   ko 'zi   'du ɾa   'sɔr te   iŋ   ko 'zi   gran   mar 'ti ɾe   laʃ: 'ʃa te mi   mo 'ri ɾe
in   così   dura   sorte,   in   così   gran   martire?   Lasciatemi   morire!
in   such   hard   fate   in   such   great   suffering   leave me   to die
against such a harsh fate, in such great suffering? Let me die!

Lasciatemi morire!

Ottavio Rinuccini

Claudio Monteverdi
edited and realized by
Alessandro Parisotti

Quella fiamma che m'accende

Benedetto Marcello
(1686-1739)

Benedetto Marcello, whose older brother Alessandro was also a composer, first studied violin with his father, but soon turned to singing and composition. In 1707 Marcello began service, through a drawing by lot, to serve on the Grand Council of the Republic in Venice, which led to further government posts as well as a legal practice, culminating in the office of Chamberlain of Brescia in 1738. Despite his governmental and legal career Marcello also managed to produce some 700 musical compositions, more than half of which feature voice and continuo. His settings of 50 Psalms of David brought him international acclaim. Marcello was known to be the anonymous author of *Il teatro alla moda*, popular satirical writings on opera that was translated into several languages.

No details are known about the origins of this particular aria. "Quella fiamma che m'accende" (with the recitative "Il mio bel foco") appeared in Parisotti's *Arie antiche* Volume 1, published by Ricordi in 1885, in the key of G minor. Parisotti's source was *Arien und Gesänge ältere Tonmeister*, edited by Carl Banck and published in 1880. Parisotti's metronomic suggestion for the aria was quarter note = 80, a tempo reflecting the romantic age of the edition and significantly slower than is commonly performed today. The Parisotti edition was published by G. Schirmer in 1894 in the *Anthology of Italian Song of the Seventeenth and Eighteenth Centuries*, later included (under the title of its recitative, "Il mio bel foco") in the 1948 Schirmer compilation *24 Italian Songs and Arias of the Seventeenth and Eighteenth Centuries*.

il	'mi o	bɛl	'fɔ ko	o	lon 'ta no	o	vi 'tʃi no	'kɛs: ser	pɔs: 'si o
Il	mio	bel	foco,	o	lontano	o	vicino	ch'esser	poss'io,
the	my	beautiful	fire	either	distant	or	near	that to be	am able I

My beautiful fire, whether I be far away or near,

'sɛn tsa	kan 'dʒar	'ma i	'tɛm pre	per	'vo i	'ka ɾe	pu 'pil: le	ar de 'ra	'sɛm pre
senza	cangiar	mai	tempre	per	voi,	care	pupille,	arderà	sempre.
without	to change	ever	strengths	for	you	dear	eyes	will burn	always

without ever changing its intensity, will burn for you, dear eyes, forever.

'kwel: la	'fjam: ma	ke	mat: 'tʃɛn de	'pja tʃe	'tan to	al: 'lal ma	'mi a
Quella	fiamma	che	m'accende	piace	tanto	all'alma	mia
that	flame	which	me ignites	is pleasing	so much	to the soul	mine

That flame which sets me on fire is so pleasing to my soul

ke	dʒam: 'ma i	se stiŋ gwe 'ra
che	giammai	s'estinguerà.
that	never	itself will extinguish

that it will never die.

e	se	il	'fa to	a	'vo i	mi	'rɛn de
E	se	il	fato	a	voi	mi	rende,
and	if	the	fate	to	you	me	gives back

And if fate returns me to you,

'va gi	'ra i	del	'mi o	bɛl	'so le
vaghi	rai	del	mio	bel	sole,
lovely	rays	of the	my	beautiful	sun

lovely rays of my beautiful sun,

'al tra	'lu tʃe	'el: la	non	'vwɔ le	ne	vo 'ler	dʒam: 'ma i	po 'tra
altra	luce	ella	non	vuole	né	voler	giammai	potrà.
other	light	it	not	wishes	nor	to wish	never	it will be able

it will not want, nor ever wish for, other light.

Quella fiamma che m'accende

Anonymous

Benedetto Marcello
edited and realized by
Carl Banck and
Alessandro Parisotti

Recitativo

Il mio bel fo - co, o lon - ta - no o vi -

ci - no ch'es-ser pos-s'i - o, sen - za can-giar mai tem - pre per

voi, ca - re pu-pil - le, ar-de - rà sem - pre.

Nel cor più non mi sento
from the opera *L'amor contrasto*

Giovanni Paisiello
(1740-1816)

Most of Paisiello's more than 80 operas are comic; he was the most successful and influential comic opera composer of his day. Born in Taranto, he was primarily educated at the Conservatorio di San Onofrio in Naples. By the late 1760s his operas rivaled Piccinni's in popularity in Naples. Paisiello's fame spread to Russia, where in 1776 he was invited to become *maestro di cappella* in the court of Catherine II in St. Petersburg. He remained there composing operas, including *Il barbiere di Siviglia* (the standard opera of that title until Rossini's 1816 score), and directing the court orchestra until 1783. He returned to Naples, where he had commissions and a court appointment. Paisiello became *maestro di cappella* nazionale when the court fled to Sicily during political battles over Naples, but was reinstated to his former royal post when the republic fell to royalists after two years. Napoleon Buonaparte admired Paisiello's music and requested his presence in Paris, where he was named director of chapel music in 1802, but returned to Naples two years later. His music remained popular in Paris, and Paisiello continued to receive French honors. Napoleon's brother Joseph became King of Naples in 1806 and Paisiello was made director of music in his court. When King Ferdinand returned to power in Naples, Paisiello, due to his service to the French, lost his court status.

"Nel cor più non mi sento" is from Paisello's tremendously popular opera *L'amor contrastato*, first produced at the Teatro dei Fiorentini in Naples in 1789. The opera was also called *La molinara* or *La bella molinara* in some of its many productions, receiving over 160 performances in Vienna alone, and remained popular throughout Europe for 40 years. The aria was sung in the opera by a soprano (with the words in this edition), then by a tenor, followed by a duet version for both characters. Many arrangements of the opera's music were made for various combinations of instruments. "Nel cor più non mi sento" was the basis for a famous set of piano variations by Beethoven.

"Nel cor più non mi sento" appeared in Parisotti's *Arie antiche* Volume 1, published by Ricordi in 1885, in the key of F major. Parisotti's metronomic suggestion was dotted quarter note = 58. Parisotti's edition was published by G. Schirmer in 1894 in the *Anthology of Italian Song of the Seventeenth and Eighteenth Centuries*, later included in the 1948 Schirmer compilation *24 Italian Songs and Arias of the Seventeenth and Eighteenth Centuries*.

nel	kɔr	pju	non	mi	'sɛn to	bril: 'lar	la	dʒo ven 'tu
Nel	cor	più	non	mi	sento	brillar	la	gioventù;
in the	heart	more	not	me	I feel	to shine	the	youth

In my heart I no longer feel youthfulness glowing;

ka 'dʒon	del	'mi o	tor 'men to	a 'mor	'sɛ i	'kol pa	tu
cagion	del	mio	tormento,	amor,	sei	colpa	tu.
cause	of the	my	torment	love	you are	fault	you

the cause of my torment, love, is your fault.

mi	'pit: tsi ki	mi	'stut: tsi ki	mi	'pun dʒi ki	mi	'ma sti ki
Mi	pizzichi,	mi	stuzzichi,	mi	pungichi,	mi	mastichi;
me	you tickle	me	you tease	me	you prick	me	you bite

You tickle me, you tease me, you prick me, you bite me;

ke	'kɔ za	ɛ	'kwe sto	a i 'mɛ	pje 'ta
che	cosa	è	questo	ahimè?	Pietà!
what	thing	is	this	alas	have pity

what is this, alas? Have pity!

a 'mo ɾe	ɛ	un	'tʃɛr to ke	ke	di spe 'ɾar	mi	fa
Amore	è	un	certo che,	che	disperar	mi	fa.
love	is	a	certain something	which	to despair	me	makes

Love is a certain something which makes me despair.

Nel cor più non mi sento

Giuseppe Palomba

Giovanni Paisiello
edited by Alessandro Parisotti

mor, sei col - pa tu. Mi piz - zi - chi, mi stuz-zi-chi, mi

pun - gi-chi, mi mas-ti-chi; che co - sa è que - sto ahi - mè?_____ Pie -

tà,_____ pie - tà,_____ pie - tà!_____ A - mo - re è un cer - to che,_____ che_

di - spe - rar_____ mi fa.

Se tu m'ami

presumably by
Alessandro Parisotti
previously attributed to
Giovanni Battista Pergolesi

"Se tu m'ami" is one of many works wrongly attributed (both deliberately and accidentally) to Giovanni Battista Pergolesi (1710-1736). During Pergolesi's short lifetime he attained little success, but following his death he was recognized as a leader in Italian comic opera. He became revered throughout Europe for the opera *La serva padrona*, which by 1755 had been performed 200 times in Paris. The *Stabat Mater* grew to enormous popularity as well. Little was known about the Italian composer that had died so young. By mid-eighteenth century Pergolesi's name had such appeal that impresarios and publishers regularly credited him with scores by unknown and little known composers in order to draw audience and sales. The practice later extended to small instrumental works. The name Pergolesi nearly became a catch-all for any anonymous work of the eighteenth century, and many spurious publications resulted with that attribution.

No manuscript of "Se tu m'ami" has been located, and it is generally agreed that the attribution to Pergolesi is spurious. Since "Se tu m'ami" was included in *Arie antiche*, edited and compiled by Alessandro Parisotti, it is presumed that Parisotti actually composed the song to an early eighteenth century text, though there is no clear evidence of this.

In a 1949 article in *Music and Letters*, "Two Centuries of Pergolesi Forgeries and Misattributions," Frank Walker states about "Se tu m'ami":

Another problem-piece! I am included to accept a suggestion by Prof. Dent that this drawing-room favorite… is really a nineteenth-century forgery. If so, it is a clever one, and the unknown forger deserves hearty congratulations. The words are from Paolo Rolli's 'Canzonette e cantata,' published in London in 1727 (Rolli provided a setting of his own), and of course, no one can now prove that a copy of this book cannot have reached Naples in Pergolesi's lifetime.

Why would Parisotti choose to attribute his original composition to Pergolesi? The practice was not unprecedented in the nineteenth century. Perhaps Parisotti was continuing the strong tradition of general attribution to Pergolesi begun in the previous century, an elaborate joke. There is an aspect of selflessness in Parisotti's decision. One also can imagine that a young man of compositional talent who had immersed himself in editing and arranging Italian music from the past simply could not resist the creative urge to write a song in the style, especially when the idea was as strong as the result proves it to be. He may not have had an opportunity to publish the song outside the volume he was editing, which could have played a part in his decision. No matter whether "Se tu m'ami" actually belongs in this collection of seventeenth and eighteenth century Italian songs, whatever its genesis, it is a gem for the ages.

Igor Stravinsky included the song in his ballet score, *Pulcinella*, based on music by Pergolesi, or on music Stravinsky believed to be by Pergolesi.

"Se tu m'ami" appeared in Parisotti's *Arie antiche* Volume 1, published by Ricordi in 1885, in the key of F minor. Parisotti's metronomic suggestion was dotted quarter note = 58, probably slower than would be aesthetically comfortable for most performances today. The song was published by G. Schirmer in 1894 in the *Anthology of Italian Song of the Seventeenth and Eighteenth Centuries*, repeating the attribution to Pergolesi, with the extended title "Se tu m'ami, se sospiri." This title and Pergolesi attribution were again used in the 1948 Schirmer publication *24 Italian Songs and Arias of the Seventeenth and Eighteenth Centuries.*

se tu	'ma mi	se tu	so 'spi ɾi	sol	per	me	dʒen 'til	pa 'stor
Se tu	**m'ami,**	**se tu**	**sospiri**	**sol**	**per**	**me,**	**gentil**	**pastor,**
if you	me you love	if you	you sigh	only	for	me	gentle	shepherd

If you love me, if you sigh only for me, gentle shepherd,

ɔ	do 'lor	de	'twɔ i	mar 'ti ɾi	ɔ	di 'lɛt: to	del	'tu o	a 'mor
ho	**dolor**	**de'**	**tuoi**	**martiri;**	**ho**	**diletto**	**del**	**tuo**	**amor,**
I have	pain	of the	your	sufferings	I have	delight	of the	your	love

I am pained by your suffering; I delight in your love,

ma se	'pɛn si	ke	so 'let: to	'i o	ti	'dɛb: ba	ri a 'mar
ma	**se**	**pensi**	**che**	**soletto**	**io**	**ti**	**debba**	**riamar,**
but	if	you think	that	all alone	I	you	ought	to love in return

but if you think I should love you alone in return,

pa sto 'rɛl: lo	'sɛ i	sod: 'dʒɛt: to	fa tʃil 'men te	a	tiŋ gan: 'nar
pastorello,	**sei**	**soggetto**	**facilmente**	**a**	**t'ingannar.**
dear shepherd	you are	subject	easily	to	yourself to deceive

dear shepherd, you are easily subject to deceiving yourself.

'bɛl: la	'rɔ za	por po 'ri na	'ɔd: dʒi	'sil vja	ʃeʎ: ʎe 'ra
Bella	**rosa**	**porporina**	**oggi**	**Silvia**	**sceglierà;**
beautiful	rose	red	today	Silvia	will choose

Today Silvia will choose a beautiful red rose;

kon	la	'sku za	'del: la	'spi na	do 'man	'pɔ i	la	spret: tse 'ra
con	**la**	**scusa**	**della**	**spina**	**doman**	**poi**	**la**	**sprezzerà.**
with	the	excuse	of the	thorn	tomorrow	then	it	she will scorn

then, with the excuse of its thorn, tomorrow she will scorn it.

ma	'deʎ: ʎi	'wɔ mi ni	il	kon 'siʎ: ʎo	'i o	per	me	non	se gwi 'rɔ
Ma	**degli**	**uomini**	**il**	**consiglio**	**io**	**per**	**me**	**non**	**seguirò.**
but	of the	men	the	advice	I	for	myself	not	I will follow

But I, for my part, will not follow the advice of men;

non	per 'ke	mi	'pja tʃe	il	'dʒiʎ: ʎo	ʎi	'al tri	'fjo ɾi	spret: tse 'rɔ
Non	**perché**	**mi**	**piace**	**il**	**giglio**	**gli**	**altri**	**fiori**	**sprezzerò.**
not	because	me	it pleases	the	lily	the	other	flowers	I will scorn

not because the lily pleases me will I scorn the other flowers.

Se tu m'ami

Paolo Antonio Rolli

presumably by
Alessandro Parisotti

Già il sole dal Gange

from the opera *L'Honestà negli amori*

Alessandro Scarlatti
(1660-1725)

Considered the most important Italian composer of his generation, Alessandro Scarlatti accomplished much for the popularity of opera during his lifetime. Born in Palermo, the second of eight children, Alessandro was sent to Rome at the age of 12, probably to live with relatives and ease the financial burden on his parents. Though details of his education are not known, he absorbed Roman musical activity. He married in 1678 and fathered eight children, though only five survived infancy. Supporting his family was an obvious priority. By 1679 Scarlatti was receiving commissions, first for an oratorio, then for an opera, *Gli equivoci nel sembiante*, a success in Rome and soon produced elsewhere. An important patron was Queen Christina of Sweden, residing in Rome, who had established two academies devoted to the arts in her palace. Scarlatti was her *maestro di cappella* until he left for Naples in 1684 to become *maestro di cappella* for the Viceroy of Naples. The composer was a major force in bringing Naples to the forefront of the opera world during the late seventeenth century. Scarlatti produced an enormous number of works in his 18 years in Naples, turning out over 40 operas as well as oratorios, cantatas, serenades and other music required for the viceroy. Political unrest in Naples caused Scarlatti to seek a position elsewhere. In 1703 he became music director at Santa Maria Maggiore in Rome. The Roman public theatres had been closed in 1700, and the musical activity of two decades before had dwindled considerably. He composed church music and music for palace concerts, though his income and position were unstable. He returned to his former position Naples in 1708 upon the invitation of a new Austrian viceroy. Though he made attempts to compose in the light comic opera style favored in Naples, it was not suited to his nature. He remained in contact with patrons in Rome and had some new operas produced as well as revivals there in 1719-1721. The final four years of his life were spent primarily in quiet retirement in Naples. Composer Domenico Scarlatti (1685-1757) was the son of Alessandro Scarlatti.

"Già il sole dal Gange" is from Scarlatti's second opera, *L'hoestà negli amori*, premiered in Rome in a private theatre at Palazzo Bernini on February 6, 1680. Bernini was the leading sculptor and architect of Rome, creating Baroque icons of the city. The aria is sung by the character Saldino as he takes in a sunrise in Algiers. The phrase "from the Ganges" refers to the sun rising from east, the direction of the famous river in India.

"Già sole dal Gange" appeared in Parisotti's *Arie antiche* Volume 2, published by Ricordi in 1890, in the key of A-flat major. Parisotti's metronomic suggestion was dotted quarter note = 126, slower than performances of today. Parisotti's edition was published by G. Schirmer in 1894 in the *Anthology of Italian Song of the Seventeenth and Eighteenth Centuries*, later included in the 1948 Schirmer compilation *24 Italian Songs and Arias of the Seventeenth and Eighteenth Centuries*.

dʒa	il	ˈso le	dal	ˈgan dʒe	pju	ˈkja ɾo	sfa ˈvil: la
Già	il	sole	dal	Gange	più	chiaro	sfavilla,
already	the	sun	from the	Ganges	more	bright	sparkles

Already the sun from the Ganges [the sunrise from the East, over the Ganges River] is sparkling brighter

e	ˈtɛr dʒe	ˈoɲ: ɲi	ˈstil: la	del: ˈlal ba	ke	ˈpjan dʒe
e	terge	ogni	stilla	dell'alba	che	piange.
and	dries	every	drop	of the dawn	which	weeps

and drying every dewdrop of the weeping dawn.

kol	ˈrad: dʒo	do ˈra to	in ˈdʒɛm: ma	ˈoɲ: ɲi	ˈstɛ lo
Col	raggio	dorato	ingemma	ogni	stelo,
with the	ray	golden	it bejewels	every	stem

With gilded ray it bejewels every stem

e	ʎi	ˈa stri	del	ˈtʃɛ lo	di ˈpin dʒe	nel	ˈpra to
e	gli	astri	del	cielo	dipinge	nel	prato.
and	the	stars	of the	heaven	it paints	in the	meadow

and paints the stars of heaven upon the meadow.

Già il sole dal Gange

Felice Parnasso

Alessandro Scarlatti
edited and realized by
Alessandro Parisotti

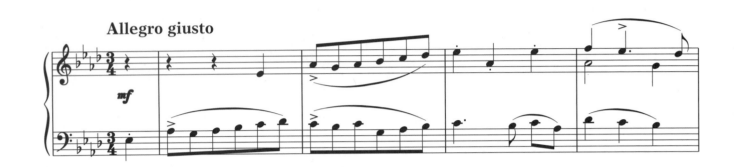

Le violette

(Rugiadose, odorose)
from the opera *Il Pirro e Demetrio*

Alessandro Scarlatti
(1660-1725)

Considered the most important Italian composer of his generation, Alessandro Scarlatti accomplished much for the popularity of opera during his lifetime. Born in Palermo, the second of eight children, Alessandro was sent to Rome at the age of 12, probably to live with relatives and ease the financial burden on his parents. Though details of his education are not known, he absorbed Roman musical activity. He married in 1678 and fathered eight children, though only five survived infancy. Supporting his family was an obvious priority. By 1679 Scarlatti was receiving commissions, first for an oratorio, then for an opera, *Gli equivoci nel sembiante*, a success in Rome and soon produced elsewhere. An important patron was Queen Christina of Sweden, residing in Rome, who had established two academies devoted to the arts in her palace. Scarlatti was her *maestro di cappella* until he left for Naples in 1684 to become *maestro di cappella* for the Viceroy of Naples. The composer was a major force in bringing Naples to the forefront of the opera world during the late seventeenth century. Scarlatti produced an enormous number of works in his 18 years in Naples, turning out over 40 operas as well as oratorios, cantatas, serenades and other music required for the viceroy. Political unrest in Naples caused Scarlatti to seek a position elsewhere. In 1703 he became music director at Santa Maria Maggiore in Rome. The Roman public theatres had been closed in 1700, and the musical activity of two decades before had dwindled considerably. He composed church music and music for palace concerts, though his income and position were unstable. He returned to his former position Naples in 1708 upon the invitation of a new Austrian viceroy. Though he made attempts to compose in the light comic opera style favored in Naples, it was not suited to his nature. He remained in contact with patrons in Rome and had some new operas produced as well as revivals there in 1719-1721. The final four years of his life were spent primarily in quiet retirement in Naples. Composer Domenico Scarlatti (1685-1757) was the son of Alessandro Scarlatti.

"Le violette" is from *Il Pirro e Demetrio*, first performed at Teatro San Bartolomeo on January 28, 1694, one of Scarlatti's more successful operas and the only one of his operas to be performed in London during his lifetime. It was retitled *La forza della fedeltà* for a Florence production of 1712. The aria is sung by a young man wondering if his love for a noble woman is folly.

"Le violette" did not appear in Parisotti's *Arie antiche*. Its source for inclusion in Schirmer's 1948 publication *24 Italian Songs and Arias of the Seventeenth and Eighteenth Centuries* is unknown. The version of the aria published there, and reproduced here, altered the form of the original.

138

ru dʒa ˈdo ze	o do ˈro ze	vi o ˈlet: te	grat: ˈtsjo ze	ˈvo i	vi ˈsta te	ver goɲ: ˈɲo ze
Rugiadose,	odorose,	violette	graziose,	voi	vi state	vergognose,
dewy	fragrant	violets	pretty	you	yourselves you stay	shy

Dewy, fragrant, pretty violets, you stay there shyly,

ˈmɛd: dzo	a ˈsko ze	fra	le	ˈfɔʎ: ʎe	e	zgri ˈda te	le	ˈmi e	ˈvɔʎ: ʎe
mezzo	ascose	fra	le	foglie,	e	sgridate	le	mie	voglie,
half	hidden	among	the	leaves	and	you rebuke	the	my	wishes

half hidden among the leaves, and rebuke my wishes,

ke	son	ˈtrɔp: po	am bit: ˈtsjo ze
che	son	troppo	ambiziose.
which	are	too	ambitious

which are too ambitious.

Le violette

Adriano Morselli

Alessandro Scarlatti

Ru-gia-do-se, o-do-ro-se, vi - o - let-te gra - zi -

o - se, ru-gia-do-se, o-do-ro-se, vi-o-let-te gra-zi -

O cessate di piagarmi
from the opera *Il Pompeo*

Alessandro Scarlatti
(1660-1725)

Considered the most important Italian composer of his generation, Alessandro Scarlatti accomplished much for the popularity of opera during his lifetime. Born in Palermo, the second of eight children, Alessandro was sent to Rome at the age of 12, probably to live with relatives and ease the financial burden on his parents. Though details of his education are not known, he absorbed Roman musical activity. He married in 1678 and fathered eight children, though only five survived infancy. Supporting his family was an obvious priority. By 1679 Scarlatti was receiving commissions, first for an oratorio, then for an opera, *Gli equivoci nel sembiante*, a success in Rome and soon produced elsewhere. An important patron was Queen Christina of Sweden, residing in Rome, who had established two academies devoted to the arts in her palace. Scarlatti was her *maestro di cappella* until he left for Naples in 1684 to become *maestro di cappella* for the Viceroy of Naples. The composer was a major force in bringing Naples to the forefront of the opera world during the late seventeenth century. Scarlatti produced an enormous number of works in his 18 years in Naples, turning out over 40 operas as well as oratorios, cantatas, serenades and other music required for the viceroy. Political unrest in Naples caused Scarlatti to seek a position elsewhere. In 1703 he became music director at Santa Maria Maggiore in Rome. The Roman public theatres had been closed in 1700, and the musical activity of two decades before had dwindled considerably. He composed church music and music for palace concerts, though his income and position were unstable. He returned to his former position Naples in 1708 upon the invitation of a new Austrian viceroy. Though he made attempts to compose in the light comic opera style favored in Naples, it was not suited to his nature. He remained in contact with patrons in Rome and had some new operas produced as well as revivals there in 1719-1721. The final four years of his life were spent primarily in quiet retirement in Naples. Composer Domenico Scarlatti (1685-1757) was the son of Alessandro Scarlatti.

"O cessate di piagarmi" is from the opera *Il Pompeo*, first performed at Teatro Colonna, a private theatre in Rome, on January 25, 1683. It was the first of many such works which Stradella based on ancient Roman history. The aria is sung by Pompey the Great to Issicratea, once the Queen of Pontus, who is held in Rome against her will.

"O cessate di piagarmi" appeared in Parisotti's *Arie antiche* Volume 1, published by Ricordi in 1885, in the key of E minor. Parisotti's metronomic suggestion was dotted quarter note = 80 for the first verse, and dotted quarter note = 50 for the second verse. Such tempo extremes between verses reflect nineteenth century sensibilities, and should be not be applied to performances today. The Parisotti edition was published by G. Schirmer in 1894 in the *Anthology of Italian Song of the Seventeenth and Eighteenth Centuries*, later included in the 1948 Schirmer compilation *24 Italian Songs and Arias of the Seventeenth and Eighteenth Centuries*.

o   tʃes: 'sa te   di   pja 'gar mi   o   laʃ: 'ʃa te mi   mo 'ɾir
O   **cessate**   **di**   **piagarmi,**   **o**   **lasciatemi**   **morir,**
either   cease   of   wounding me   or   leave me   to die
Either stop wounding me or let me die,

'lu tʃiŋ 'gra te   di spje 'ta te   pju   del   'dʒɛ lo   e   pju   'de i   'mar mi
luc'ingrate,   **dispietate,**   **più**   **del**   **gelo**   **e**   **più**   **dei**   **marmi**
eyes ungrateful   pitiless   more   than the   ice   and   more   than the   marbles
ungrateful eyes, pitiless, more than ice and more than marble

'fred: de   e   'sor de   a   'mjɛ i   mar 'tir
fredde   **e**   **sorde**   **a'**   **miei**   **martir.**
cold   and   deaf   to   my   suffering
cold and deaf to my suffering.

O cessate di piagarmi

Nicola Minato

Alessandro Scarlatti
edited and realized by
Alessandro Parisotti

*La seconda volta
molto ritenuto*

Se Florindo è fedele
from the opera *La donna ancora è fedele*

Alessandro Scarlatti
(1660-1725)

Considered the most important Italian composer of his generation, Alessandro Scarlatti accomplished much for the popularity of opera during his lifetime. Born in Palermo, the second of eight children, Alessandro was sent to Rome at the age of 12, probably to live with relatives and ease the financial burden on his parents. Though details of his education are not known, he absorbed Roman musical activity. He married in 1678 and fathered eight children, though only five survived infancy. Supporting his family was an obvious priority. By 1679 Scarlatti was receiving commissions, first for an oratorio, then for an opera, *Gli equivoci nel sembiante*, a success in Rome and soon produced elsewhere. An important patron was Queen Christina of Sweden, residing in Rome, who had established two academies devoted to the arts in her palace. Scarlatti was her *maestro di cappella* until he left for Naples in 1684 to become *maestro di cappella* for the Viceroy of Naples. The composer was a major force in bringing Naples to the forefront of the opera world during the late seventeenth century. Scarlatti produced an enormous number of works in his 18 years in Naples, turning out over 40 operas as well as oratorios, cantatas, serenades and other music required for the viceroy. Political unrest in Naples caused Scarlatti to seek a position elsewhere. In 1703 he became music director at Santa Maria Maggiore in Rome. The Roman public theatres had been closed in 1700, and the musical activity of two decades before had dwindled considerably. He composed church music and music for palace concerts, though his income and position were unstable. He returned to his former position Naples in 1708 upon the invitation of a new Austrian viceroy. Though he made attempts to compose in the light comic opera style favored in Naples, it was not suited to his nature. He remained in contact with patrons in Rome and had some new operas produced as well as revivals there in 1719-1721. The final four years of his life were spent primarily in quiet retirement in Naples. Composer Domenico Scarlatti (1685-1757) was the son of Alessandro Scarlatti.

"Se Florindo è fedele" is from the opera *La donna ancora è fedele*, first performed in Naples at Teatro San Bartolomeo in 1698. The character Alidoro sings it after learning that Florinda loves him. Parisotti changed Florinda (a woman) to Florindo (a man) in his edition. A male singing this song could change "Florindo" to "Florinda," which also changes the song title, of course.

"Se Florindo è fedele" appeared in Parisotti's *Arie antiche* Volume 1, published by Ricordi in 1885, in the key of A-flat major. Parisotti's metronomic suggestion was eighth note = 132, slower than a common tempo for this aria today. The Parisotti edition was published by G. Schirmer in 1894 in the *Anthology of Italian Song of the Seventeenth and Eighteenth Centuries*, later included in the 1948 Schirmer compilation *24 Italian Songs and Arias of the Seventeenth and Eighteenth Centuries*.

se   flo ˈrin do   ɛ   fe ˈde le   ˈi o   min: na mo ɾe ˈrɔ
Se   Florindo   è   fedele   io   m'innamorerò.
if   Florindo   is   faithful   I   myself will fall in love
If Florindo is faithful, I will fall in love.

po ˈtra   bɛn   ˈlar ko   ˈtɛn de ɾe   il   fa ɾe ˈtra to   ar ˈtʃɛr
Potrà   ben   l'arco   tendere   il   faretrato   arcier,
will be able   well   the bow   to stretch   the   quiver-bearing   archer
The archer, armed with quiver, may well draw his bow,

ˈki o   mi   sa ˈprɔ   di ˈfɛn de ɾe   dun   ˈgwar do   lu ziŋ ˈgjɛr
ch'io   mi   saprò   difendere   d'un   guardo   lusinghier.
because I   myself   I will know how   to defend   from a   glance   flattering
for I will know how to defend myself from a flattering glance.

ˈprɛ gi   ˈpjan ti   e   kwe ˈrɛ le   ˈi o   non   a skol te ˈrɔ
Preghi,   pianti   e   querele   io   non   ascolterò,
entreaties   tears   and   complaints   I   not   I will listen to
I will not listen to entreaties, weeping and complaints;

ma   se   sa ˈra   fe ˈde le   ˈi o   min: na mo ɾe ˈrɔ
ma   se   sarà   fedele   io   m'innamorerò.
but   if   he will be   faithful   I   myself will fall in love
but if he is faithful, I will fall in love.

Se Florindo* è fedele

Domenico Filippo Contini

Alessandro Scarlatti
edited and realized by
Alessandro Parisotti

Allegretto grazioso, moderato assai

Se Flo - rin - do è fe - de - le io m'in - na - mo - re - rò, se Flo - rin - do è fe - de - le io m'in - na -

* A male singer may change this to "Florinda."

Sento nel core

Alessandro Scarlatti
(1660-1725)

Considered the most important Italian composer of his generation, Alessandro Scarlatti accomplished much for the popularity of opera during his lifetime. Born in Palermo, the second of eight children, Alessandro was sent to Rome at the age of 12, probably to live with relatives and ease the financial burden on his parents. Though details of his education are not known, he absorbed Roman musical activity. He married in 1678 and fathered eight children, though only five survived infancy. Supporting his family was an obvious priority. By 1679 Scarlatti was receiving commissions, first for an oratorio, then for an opera, *Gli equivoci nel sembiante*, a success in Rome and soon produced elsewhere. An important patron was Queen Christina of Sweden, residing in Rome, who had established two academies devoted to the arts in her palace. Scarlatti was her *maestro di cappella* until he left for Naples in 1684 to become *maestro di cappella* for the Viceroy of Naples. The composer was a major force in bringing Naples to the forefront of the opera world during the late seventeenth century. Scarlatti produced an enormous number of works in his 18 years in Naples, turning out over 40 operas as well as oratorios, cantatas, serenades and other music required for the viceroy. Political unrest in Naples caused Scarlatti to seek a position elsewhere. In 1703 he became music director at Santa Maria Maggiore in Rome. The Roman public theatres had been closed in 1700, and the musical activity of two decades before had dwindled considerably. He composed church music and music for palace concerts, though his income and position were unstable. He returned to his former position Naples in 1708 upon the invitation of a new Austrian viceroy. Though he made attempts to compose in the light comic opera style favored in Naples, it was not suited to his nature. He remained in contact with patrons in Rome and had some new operas produced as well as revivals there in 1719-1721. The final four years of his life were spent primarily in quiet retirement in Naples. Composer Domenico Scarlatti (1685-1757) was the son of Alessandro Scarlatti.

"Sento nel core" is from a short cantata, a Baroque form for voice and continuo, comprised of arias or arioso and recitative, or for combinations of solos, duets, ensembles and sometimes chorus for more elaborate works. In seventeenth century Italy a cantata was specifically for solo voice and basso continuo and intended for small, private performances. Late in the century the da capo aria figured prominently in solo cantatas.

"Sento nel core" appeared in Parisotti's *Arie antiche* Volume 2, published by Ricordi in 1890, in the key of F minor. Parisotti's metronomic suggestion was quarter note = 76, slower than performances of today. Parisotti's edition was published by G. Schirmer in 1894 in the *Anthology of Italian Song of the Seventeenth and Eighteenth Centuries*.

'sɛn to	nel	'kɔ ɾe	'tʃɛr to	do 'lo ɾe	ke	la	'mi a	'pa tʃe	tur 'ban do	va
Sento	nel	core	certo	dolore	che	la	mia	pace	turbando	va.
I feel	in the	heart	certain	pain	which	the	my	peace	disturbing	goes

I feel in my heart a certain pain which disturbs my peace.

'splɛn de	'u na	'fa tʃe	ke	'lal ma	at: 'tʃɛn de	se	non	ɛ	a 'mo ɾe	a 'mor	sa 'ra
Splende	una	face	che	l'alma	accende;	se	non	è	amore,	amor	sarà.
shines	a	torch	which	the soul	ignites	if	not	is	love	love	will be

A torch shines, which ignites my soul; if it is not love, love it will be.

Sento nel core

Anonymous

Alessandro Scarlatti
edited and realized by
Alessandro Parisotti

Sen - to nel co - re cer - to do - lo - re, cer - to do -

lo - re che la mia pa - ce ___ tur - ban - do ___

va, nel co - re, nel

se non è a - mo - re, _____ a - mor _____ sa - rà.

Sen - to nel

co - re cer - to do - lo - re, cer - to do - lo - re

che la mia pa - ce _____ tur - ban - do va,

Tu lo sai

Giuseppe Torelli
(1658-1709)

Giuseppe Torelli is best known as a composer of instrumental music, with some 150 compositions to his credit. He was important in the development of the Baroque concerto, both solo concerto and concerto grosso. Torelli composed few vocal works, and no operas. Little is known of his early training in Verona, the city of his birth. He was admitted to the Accademia Filarmonica in Bologna in 1684. Torelli was a noted violin virtuoso, and made most of his living at that instrument. After leaving Bologna in 1696 he spent four years in Vienna, after which he traveled extensively, primarily in Italy, and died in Bologna in 1709.

Nothing is known about the aria "Tu lo sai," but it was probably an individual composition with continuo, not excerpted from a larger work. Albert Fuchs edited the aria and included it in the 1901 publication *Bel Canto*, which was the source for Lester Hodges' 1948 Schirmer compilation *24 Italian Songs and Arias of the Seventeenth and Eighteenth Centuries*.

tu	lo	'sa i		'kwan to	ta 'ma i	tu	lo	'sa i	kru 'dɛl
Tu	**lo**	**sai**		**quanto**	**t'amai;**	**tu**	**lo**	**sai,**	**crudel!**
you	it	you know		how much	you I loved	you	it	you know	cruel one

You know how much I loved you; you know it, cruel one!

'i o	non	'bra mo	'al tra	mer 'tʃe	ma	ri 'kɔr da ti		di	me
Io	**non**	**bramo**	**altra**	**mercé,**	**ma**	**ricordati**		**di**	**me,**
I	not	I desire	other	mercy	but	may remember you		of	me

I wish no other mercy than that you remember me

e	'pɔ i	'sprɛt: tsa	un	in fe 'del
e	**poi**	**sprezza**	**un**	**infedel!**
and	then	despise	an	unfaithful one

and then despise an unfaithful one!

Tu lo sai

Anonymous

Giuseppe Torelli
edited and realized by
Albert Fuchs and
Lester Hodges

Tu lo _____ sai quan - to t'a - mai; _____ tu lo _____
sai, lo sai, _____ cru - del! _____ Io non bra - mo
al - tra mer - cé, ma ri - cor - da - ti di me,

* The following introduction, an editorial suggestion, may be used:

e poi sprez - za un — in - fe - del, e poi

sprez - za un — in - fe - del! Tu lo — sai

quan - to t'a - mai; — tu lo — sai, lo sai, — cru - del, —

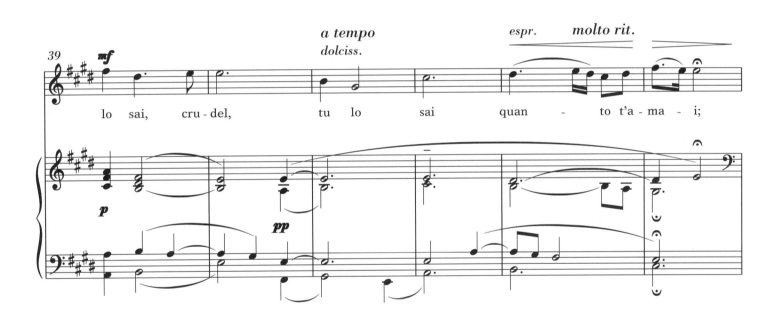

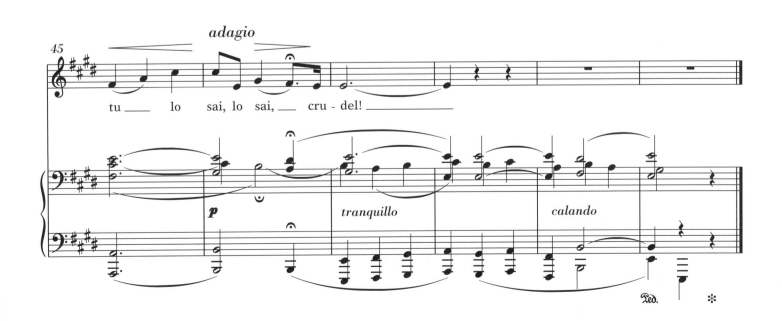